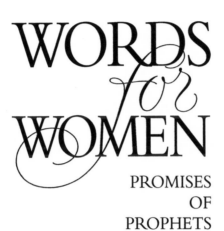

WORDS for WOMEN

PROMISES
OF
PROPHETS

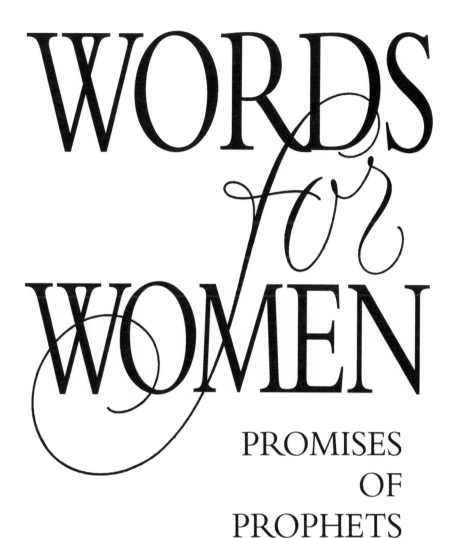

WORDS for WOMEN

PROMISES OF PROPHETS

BARBARA B. SMITH

SHIRLEY W. THOMAS

BOOKCRAFT
Salt Lake City, Utah

Library of Congress Catalog Card Number: 94-70745
ISBN 0-88494-921-4

First Printing, 1994

Printed in the United States of America

CONTENTS

PROLOGUE:
IN KEEPING WITH A PROMISE

*I*nstruction from the Prophet Joseph Smith was an important component of the first meeting of the Female Relief Society of Nauvoo on March 17, 1842. The meeting came about because the women of the newly established Church desired to form a society to help the cause of Zion by making shirts for the brethren working on the temple and by attending to the wants of the many new converts arriving daily in the city. Learning of their expressed interest, the Prophet met with a group of twenty sisters and two other brethren in the lodge room over his store, where he organized them after a pattern of the priesthood and gave them his prophetic approval. Of this meeting he wrote, in part, "I gave much instruction."[1]

Instruction from the Lord through his appointed priesthood leaders has been a distinguishing characteristic and a guiding influence of the Society since that day. As the Prophet said in a lengthy discourse to the women on April 28, 1842, "You will receive instructions through the order of the Priesthood which God has established, through the medium of those appointed to lead."[2]

In keeping with that promise, instruction by a designated General Authority is now given at each Relief Society general meeting and published in the *Ensign,* where it becomes a continuing resource. Earlier talks, however, are not so readily available.

Before the reorganization of the Church magazines and lesson manuals and the revised production of Church materials in the 1970s, the Relief Society had for many years published the *Relief Society Magazine*. It was here that priesthood leaders' talks to the sisters were printed.

While the current instruction of the brethren provides obvious vitality to the Relief Society—a prophetic voice responding to the present need of the sisters—still there is much of worth in the talks that have been given in past years. In both precept and promise they offer a resource of strength that yet has value. This volume contains selected passages from General Authorities' talks that have been preserved in the pages of the *Relief Society Magazine*. Along with these, the book includes illustrative experiences from the lives of Relief Society women, experiences that point to the influence that instructions of the brethren can have in the lives of the sisters. Although the addresses of the brethren reflect the times in which they were given, such as the Great Depression, a world war, an expanding Church, they contain lasting gospel truths that are for all time. They are given here as a legacy to the women of the Church, a part of a Prophet's promise.

1

THE INDIVIDUAL
IS SUPREME

---

*In Mormon philosophy, the individual is supreme under the God
of heaven.*

—*Ezra Taft Benson*

*O*ur sisters are entitled just as
much to the inspiration for their needs of the Holy Spirit as are
the men, every bit," said President Joseph Fielding Smith at the
1959 Relief Society conference.[1] In the pages of this book are
some of the inspired words offered to women "for their needs."
They are drawn from talks that brethren of the leading councils
of the Church gave to the Relief Society—this Society whose
program, pointed out Elder Gordon B. Hinckley, "came under
the inspiration of the Prophet for the blessing of women
throughout the earth."[2]

No fundamental need is addressed more frequently in these
speeches than the need for appreciation and acceptance. Typical
are the words of President Heber J. Grant, who said that his heart
was full of gratitude to Heavenly Father "for the faithfulness and
devotion of the sisters of Relief Society."[3] Representative also are
these words of Elder Melvin J. Ballard: "God bless you sisters for
what you have done—a noble work."[4] In a similar vein, Elder
Mark E. Petersen said: "I would like to join, my sisters, with

President Joseph Fielding Smith, in expressing gratitude and appreciation to you for all that you do."5 Such positive remarks as these provide a consistent message given throughout the talks.

While it is likely that the sisters would not have stated a need for such expressions of appreciation—nor perhaps even have been aware of a need—the frequency with which the Brethren give the sisters commendation and thanks and the inspired nature of the talks suggest that there is in these statements a sacred purpose—a divine wisdom—that before advice can be well received a human spirit needs acceptance. And in these addresses acceptance has been freely given to the sisters. The very recurrence of its expression provides a context of loving respect in which all other instructions were given.

As a godly attribute, the expressing of deserved praise has ready application, and receiving approval, even in small ways, is vital to providing an atmosphere in which an individual's respect for self can thrive. Note the seeming insignificance of the following commonplace incident: A young married sister, after visiting with a group of Relief Society women, said good-bye to them and went on her way. When the young sister was just out of hearing, one of the remaining women remarked that the young sister's hair was especially pretty. Others agreed. But the one who knew the young sister best said, "It is too bad you didn't say that when she was here. She needs to know that you admire her."

Many can relate to this true episode—maybe see themselves in the place of the young sister—but some of the women in the group recognized in the wiser woman's comment a principle: appreciation truly felt can bless others when it is communicated. If sincerely done, this practice places within our reach a means of affecting another person's life positively. It is good to remember that when Heavenly Father is well pleased he expresses it. Observe how often he speaks it, for example, when introducing his Son: "This is my beloved Son, in whom I am well pleased" (Matthew 3:17).

In addition to expressing appreciation, when speaking to Relief Society conferences the brethren addressed widely ranging topics relating to the gospel, giving advice, caution, or encouragement as they were inspired. Although the subjects varied with the circumstances of the world or of the Church, the words were spoken with the intent to serve the women—more particularly, *each* woman. For while there was a great deal to be talked of and taught—about the home, about families, and about the work of the Society itself—the brethren had no doubt of the truth that the individual woman is the critical component to the success of the Relief Society.

Although the family is clearly fundamental in working out the plan of salvation, the individual is the key figure. Whether we are married or single, when we are grown the responsibility for our spiritual growth is ultimately our own.

One sister, after losing her husband of fifty-two years, wrote: "Kindness and concern do help ease the aching heart. [He] is well again and in a happy place. . . . We had 52-plus years together, and they were wonderful years. . . . We come into this world one at a time and leave the same way." Through her words we can feel her pain at a temporary separation from her husband, but we can also sense the strength that has come to her from the gospel's sustaining power and from her knowledge that although she is now alone she is nevertheless whole. As close and as long as a marriage can be, peace in our lives comes through our own faith, our personal belief, our individual commitment.

The Church teaches strongly the value of marriage and good families; they are necessary for receiving and nurturing the spirit children who come to earth. But marriages work best when individuals have a wholesome understanding of who they are and of who they can become; when they are prepared to contribute to as well as receive from a partnership; and when they have a "self" to lose in the service of others. The same preparation equips a person to live well singly.

The Savior was reared as a child in the family of Joseph and Mary, with a father to teach him a trade, and parents to wonder where he was when they could not find him in the family caravan. Then he grew to function as an individual. On one occasion

Jesus was informed that his mother and brethren wanted to speak to him, and the Master answered, "Who is my mother? and who are my brethren?" (Matthew 12:48.) We would be remiss to conclude from these words that he had lost all feeling for his family; we know that he had not. But whatever else he may have meant, Jesus did teach through those words that discipleship is more a matter of faith than of family—as important as the latter is.

When Elder Ezra Taft Benson said that "in Mormon philosophy, the individual is supreme,"[6] he did not mean that Latter-day Saints celebrate the single life but that a person is saved as an individual. Therefore, programs of the Church are geared to the needs of the one. Relief Society visiting teachers are given individual sisters to learn to know, to serve, and to care about. They see to the needs of that sister in a one-to-one way. It is significant that a woman often refers to her visiting teachers as "*my* visiting teacher." And each sister has one—two, actually. This is particularly important to the woman who lives alone yet who knows that there is always someone who is available to her and concerned about her.

So, while in their talks given at the Relief Society conferences the brethren addressed all of the women, undoubtedly it was their hope that their words might help individual sisters. Many of these conference addresses were discourses on principles of the gospel, some dealt with the relationships women might experience, and some reflected conditions of the world that could have an impact on the lives of Latter-day Saint women. One of the times when the brethren seemed especially concerned about the sisters and changes affecting their lives was at the close of World War II.

In one talk, President J. Reuben Clark, Jr., made reference to Daniel Webster's observation that a mariner, after enduring a heavy storm, when the sky once again appeared through the clouds, always quickly took the opportunity to get his bearings, to see where he was.[7]

In a similar way, at the end of the war in the mid 1940s, women, looking about, found a very different view than they had seen before. During the years of the conflict it had been necessary for them to help man the war effort, which meant their often performing services that would have previously been considered unsuitable for them; they also earned wages not known before. When the war was over, the result—and it was almost irreversible—was that women were now doing what once had been called man's work, and many women were loath to leave their jobs.

These conditions affected members of the Church; and, with a doctrine that points to a long view of life, Latter-day Saint women needed to reassess and to determine if a new course would lead to their eternal goals. This was a time not only for reflection but also for inspired guidance—and it came. It was pertinent to that time, and it is applicable today.

President David O. McKay gave specific focus to the matter of women working in nontraditional vocations. Although the role he described with regard to the sisters was not a limited one, his words do contain—as the Prophet Joseph Smith promised—important counsel:

> I don't know that there is any objection to women entering the fields of literature, science, art, social economy, . . . and all kinds of learning, or participation in any and all things which contribute to the fulness of her womanhood and increase her upbuilding influence in the world; but I do know that there are three areas or realms in which women's influence should always be felt. No matter what changes take place, these three realms should be dominated always by the beauty, the virtue, and intelligence of womankind.
>
> I should like to refer to those three: The first . . . is the realm of home building. Next to that is the realm of teaching, and the third, . . . the realm of compassionate service.[8]

One sister's life seemed to reflect the spirit of President McKay's counsel. Educated to be an attorney, she skillfully brought her law school training to bear on her marriage and, later, her motherhood. As a new graduate, the law at first seemed all-engrossing. Even with her marriage this changed little, because she and her husband shared that interest. But with the birth of their first child, she gained a greater understanding of her role as a woman and of her legal training.

Her schooling in advocacy suddenly had its most important application. She saw her maternal relationship to their little son as that of advocate; she was his defender, his counselor, his protector to the world. She was happy now in her home with a "case" more important than any she had ever had. Long a Church member, she came to appreciate Relief Society while she was a student. Now all the preparations came together in sublime fulfillment. She would have her realm of home building "dominated by the beauty, virtue, and intelligence of womankind."

Further instruction came from President Hugh B. Brown, who said to the sisters, in a tone of encouragement: "Get the most possible service out of your time, your body, and your brain, and let all your efforts be directed into honorable channels that no effort shall be wasted and no labor result in loss or evil. Seek the very best society, be kind, polite, agreeable, seeking always to learn whatever is good."[9]

President Brown's counsel to consider what one receives in exchange for time and effort holds strong today. Prophetic advice and our prayerful consideration are needed because it is so easily possible for us to make choices, then find our labor has resulted in loss.

This happened with one woman who learned later on how deeply she regretted the way she had spent her time and her brain. Now a highly respected corporate executive, she told a committee planning a conference for a national women's organization that she hoped they would stress concerns of family and home. She and her husband thought they had provided well for their daughter by giving her the best of child care, clothes, lessons, and schools, while they focused their energies on succeeding in the corporate world. When this woman had reached her goal of career success, she wanted to enjoy it with her daughter, but found her daughter had no interest. The daughter told her mother, "When I needed and wanted your company, you were not available, and now my life is filled with activities that do not include you." The woman was heartsick, for she knew what her eighteen-year-old daughter said was true, and she could not call back those years.

As Latter-day Saint women with an understanding of the eternal possibility for families, we can make wiser choices with more rewarding results. When things in our lives do go amiss, we are thankful for the power of the Atonement, but we are also thankful for prophets who counsel us, "Get the most possible service out of your time, your body, and your brain."

Elder George Albert Smith's words of counsel were as practical as they were specific: "Your strength is not in might but in the power of righteousness. . . . No matter where you work or in what manner you serve, be sure that you keep your word. Give 100 per cent service and always be dependable. Once you have accepted an assignment, no matter how large or small, never fail to perform your part. . . . Anchor your faith in God. Be helpful, prayerful, humble and full of courage."[10]

The ample advice given to women regarding their place in the post-war world was not so much for the hope that they would have good jobs with adequate pay, or that they would decide not to work at all, but for a more far-reaching reason. The inspired brethren were concerned that the choices made by the sisters would lead to their salvation, to the saving of their souls.

Saving souls is at the heart of the gospel message. It is also a fundamental assignment of the Relief Society. The Prophet Joseph Smith stated plainly: "The Ladies' Relief Society is not only to relieve the poor, but to save souls."[11]

Elder Marion G. Romney, in a precise explanation to the sisters, told what is meant by the soul and how it can be saved. Brief sections are included here, in words that are almost deceptively plain for a truth that is both exalted and profound:

> [The] scriptures teach that a soul is saved by being brought back into the "kingdom of God."

What he was speaking about when he used the word "soul," the Lord explained by saying ". . . the spirit and the body are the soul of man." (D&C 88:15.) . . .

. . . When a mother gives birth to a child, a human soul—a spirit child of God in a mortal body—is born.

This is the answer to the Psalmist's query: "What is man . . . ?" (Ps. 8:4.) . . .

And so I repeat—an indispensable prerequisite to saving souls is an ever-present consciousness of what a soul is, what it means to save it, and how one may be saved.[12]

The opportunity to help save a soul may come in a guise as unexpected as a pair of blue jeans. At the Relief Society section of a regional meeting, a question was raised about proper dress in the then weekday Relief Society meetings. There was a lively exchange about how different groups had handled this matter. Then one particularly attractive president spoke. Given her well-dressed appearance, she might have been expected to speak in favor of a strict dress code, but she quite surprised the group by telling them that the first time she ever came to Relief Society, to a homemaking meeting, she was wearing a tee shirt and blue jeans. She said that, had someone told her then that her dress was not appropriate, she likely would never have come back.

This stopped all discussion. It was clear to everyone that although a feeling of refinement would always be appropriate in meetings, the value of an individual woman's soul was far too great to risk offending her because of her attire.

The experience of this sister underscores the truth stated by Elder Thomas S. Monson regarding the primary role of the Church: "The personal exaltation of the individual is paramount. Meetings become not an end in themselves, but the means to the desired end."[13]

The refining, soul-saving functions of Relief Society could be seen here in process—not only in the example of how continued attendance and participation may have guided the president who told about her tee shirt and dungarees, but also as the others present at the regional meeting were learning to temper judgments and heighten their sensitivities.

Elder Gordon B. Hinckley told of his opportunity to observe Relief Society's effect upon women of many cultures:

> And then to see . . . the marvelous miracles that occur to those women [in the Far East] when the light of the gospel touches their lives and the blessings of Relief Society bring new knowledge, new ambition, new hope, and new accomplishment. Their economic circumstances may not improve substantially, but their entire outlook is altered. Life becomes more than survival; it becomes purposeful. . . .
>
> . . . I would hope that I might, in some small measure, increase your appreciation for the development that will come to any woman who will take advantage of the challenges and responsibilities of Relief Society activity. . . . Four great fields of opportunity [are] afforded you and your associates throughout the world under this remarkable program. They are:
>
> 1. Strengthening the home
> 2. Enriching the mind
> 3. Subduing self
> 4. Feeding the spirit. . . .
>
> No woman could for long mingle with a group of Relief Society sisters, serve with them, pray with them, hear their testimonies, and study with them the word of the Lord, without growing in faith.[14]

Elder Hinckley then told of meeting a woman who—although at that time an active and enthusiastic member of the Church, a member missionary, and a capable business woman—had been at one time disillusioned with life, hardened, blasé, and a chain-smoker. Elder Hinckley said of her, "She credits two major factors in the miraculous change that has come over her—reading The Book of Mormon and activity in the Relief Society—The Book of Mormon which gave birth to her faith, and the Relief Society which nurtured it."[15]

In this same talk, Elder Hinckley described a scene that demonstrates how, worldwide, Relief Society can help each woman who is touched by its sacred sisterhood:

Sister Hinckley and I walked one day into a classroom . . . in Taipei, in the Republic of China. The room was cold, the furnishings were meager. A group of Relief Society sisters were studying a lesson. We could not fathom the Mandarin Chinese in which they spoke, but we could understand from the appearance of their intelligent faces what was going on.

They were thinking, and they were growing, these mature, wonderful Chinese women whose minds were being opened on a new window of great thoughts.[16]

Just as surely as Relief Society opened the minds of those Chinese women, so Relief Society women in Salt Lake City had new awakenings. One sister volunteered for an assignment to help Vietnamese women settle into the community. The sister went to a home where she found a woman who was not a member of the Church (as most others were) but who did need help. The woman was Catholic and had not yet been able to find a Catholic priest. The Relief Society sister made numerous inquiries and finally put her in touch with the appropriate cleric. The Vietnamese woman seemed to realize that the Relief Society sister had gone to some lengths to be certain that her needs had been met. She appreciated this. Although her need for help is past, she remains in contact with the Relief Society sister because she enjoys their friendship.

Sometimes the new realization is not person-to-person but just a knowledge that someone needs what the sisters can provide. Many Relief Society women keep a very large ball of cotton thread handy for any minutes they can spend crocheting bandages for lepers in some faraway place. The hand-crocheted bandages have particular qualities of stretchability, air penetration, and washability that make them especially suitable for wrapping the limbs of these patients. However, since bandages made for adults need to be nine feet long, and even those for children four or five feet long, by the time the bandages near completion the women making them are carrying a lot of material around. But as they ply their hooks, some of the difficulties they face seem less. Their thoughts turn to other problems and people, and they have pleasure in the knowledge that they can help.

One sister—like so many who have grown through Relief Society participation—was called to a teaching assignment and felt a need to study extensively to prepare. She read the manual many times, the suggested references, found more books and read those. Long burdened with a sense of inadequacy rooted in the lack of advanced schooling, the sister grasped this assignment as an opportunity. As she did, she found that her limitations lessened with purposeful study. Her confidence grew and so did her enthusiasm. She became so caught up in her study that her family was influenced. Because of her study, one son gained an interest that determined his college major.

The woman and her husband attended a dinner for business associates of her husband. One of them, an executive from the home office, conversed with her for most of the evening. Finally he asked, "Where did you study?" She knew his question implied respect for her knowledge. Thinking he wouldn't relate to Relief Society, she said simply, "I read quite a lot." But his question was for her a fulfillment. Her desire for learning was being satisfied. She knew she could continue to acquire that for which she had felt a need. An even more rewarding growth came in her increased sense of well-being. She was able to see more clearly who she was and who she could become.

Elder Marion G. Romney urged the sisters to help others to "understand and appreciate that they are, individually, in very deed, the children of God; members of his eternal family; that they . . . have the potential . . . to be like him." Speaking then as if to each sister, Elder Romney promised: "Get these truths imbedded in your minds. If you will do that, you will have an anchor that will carry you over the roughest passages in your lives."[17]

As large as the Church is and ever will become, and as broad as the scope of every nation and kindred can include, the gospel is still for the one. Relief Society reaches out to all sisters, with an intent to bless each life and save each soul.

In a quietly confident statement, President N. Eldon Tanner gave further focus to the individual as he said, "I wish to assure you that if you take this gospel seriously, and you must, into your homes and each of you live it every day in your community, your influence will be felt and you will be filling your mission."[18]

2

TAKING HOLD OF
THE TRUTH

Receive the truth, and take the Holy Spirit for your guide.
—Marion G. Romney

*P*rophets testify of blessings the Lord has for each of us to enjoy. The prophet Lehi, for example, stated plainly, "Men are, that they might have joy" (2 Nephi 2:25). The Lord provides the way that such joy may be found, but it remains with the agency of each individual to receive what is offered.

Claiming the blessings is our part. This was deeply impressed upon many sisters one day in the board room of the Relief Society Building. The year 1982 marked one hundred and forty years since the organization of Relief Society, and the general presidency and general board planned a celebration to honor the occasion. The event grew; the Young Women and Primary General Boards joined with Relief Society in what became known as "Legacy Remembered and Renewed," a tribute to women. With concerts, an art show, a walking tour, a reception, open houses, a broadcast, and more, it was to be an undertaking larger than any previously attempted. And the time was very short in which to bring it all into being. The General Authority advisor, Elder Dean L. Larsen, offered to meet with the combined presidencies and boards and ask the Lord for the powers of heaven to aid the efforts of the sisters.

He gave a beautiful blessing that included petition for needed help and direction. The women were pleased and felt this benediction would ensure their success. Then, when he finished, Elder Larsen said, "This is my faith and the Lord's desire, but now you must go and claim the blessings."

The opportunities and possibilities were abundantly there, and the Lord was ready to bless. Now it was for the sisters to bring the blessings to pass through their faith and efforts.

It is the same when it comes to partaking of the goodness of the gospel. The Lord provides the possibilities and will do all he can, but we must receive. We must claim the blessings. We begin by believing that God is and that we are his children.

President N. Eldon Tanner offered this instruction: "There is nothing that would give [individuals] greater strength and desire to live as they should than actually to know that they are the spirit children of God and to know that the spark of divinity which is within them makes their potentials and possibilities unlimited; and then to know that God actually lives, that he and his Son Jesus Christ are interested in us, and that the gospel is the plan of life and salvation which will give us the greatest joy and success."[1]

Remarkable transformations occur in the lives of people when these truths become certainties to them. Their motivation and their priorities change, choices matter more, and they live differently.

While traveling on a Church assignment, one dedicated Latter-day Saint remarked to her companion that the gospel had not always been the focus of her life, that on a Sunday morning she might have been as easily found on a tennis court as on her way to a Church meeting.

Asked what made her change, she gave the unusual reply, "I learned that when I prayed, there was someone there." Then she related the following sequence of events: Even though she had not been active, she was a known member of the Church. Because she was a member (and was kind and caring by nature) the missionaries often stopped by her home. They appreciated her cooking, but were also concerned for her soul.

When a General Authority came to visit the area, a special missionary meeting was to be held, and the Elders asked if she would transport a group of them there in her van. She willingly did, but when they arrived the missionaries wanted her to come in. After much protesting, she finally agreed to sit in the back of the chapel.

What she heard that day stirred in her some almost forgotten emotions. After the speaker finished, but before the meeting was over, she slipped out. Alone in her van, she prayed. She wanted to know if what she was beginning to feel again was of the Lord and if, in fact, her prayer was heard. The answer came, and although she has not felt it appropriate to share the details of her experience with others, it was of such intensity that she has never again wavered in her faith.

The Savior said, "My sheep hear my voice" (John 10:27). This sister heard it as she sat in the back of the chapel; it was confirmed in what she felt as she knelt alone in her van.

One day while tending a year-old grandson, one grandmother saw how compellingly a voice can bond two souls. She relates: "He had been contented with his grandfather and me, going inquisitively from one cupboard to another or to one table decoration or another, pulling out everything. Then a door opened and closed and he heard his mother's voice call him by name. Those chubby, still wobbly little legs went just as fast as they could. His arms stretched wide, and a big smile beamed on that little face, his dark eyes bright with happiness. When he reached her, she scooped him up and held him close. She kissed him and spoke tender words of love as he buried his face securely in her shoulder."

How many times have you witnessed a similar reaction as a child recognized a sweet, familiar voice and then joined in a heartwarming reunion?

The grandmother continued: "In that instant my grandson took me back to a lesson I learned while visiting Jerusalem. A friend who had already visited the Holy Land had repeatedly described how she watched several flocks of sheep intermingle while their shepherds visited together. When it was time for the shepherds to go, she thought they would never get the sheep divided and back to the right shepherd. Instead, almost miraculously, they divided themselves at the sound of each shepherd's voice.

"Because this remarkable phenomenon had been described to me, I watched for it. It happened—just as my friend had described. I was fascinated. I inquired how the sheep could possibly hear the voice of their own shepherd and recognize it from the other shepherds' voices. It was then I gained new insight. I was told that when the lambs were little each shepherd carried them often, speaking softly to them, so that when the time came for each lamb to be on its own, it would know and respond to its shepherd's voice."

It was so with the woman who slipped out of the missionary meeting and knelt in her van that day. Whatever her personal experience might have been, she heard the Shepherd's voice. It spoke so unmistakably to her heart that she has not turned from the truth she there came to realize. In the years that have followed, she has been a committed member and devoted worker in the Church. Her family's life is also centered around the gospel. The power of *her* faith is reflected in the strength of *their* testimonies. The joy of the Lord is mirrored in the happiness of their family.

Her life is witness to the truths spoken by President George Albert Smith: "We have no way of measuring the blessings of the Lord unless we live so that we can enjoy them. . . . There are certain requirements that we must observe if we are to enjoy all that we should enjoy."[2]

"All that we should enjoy" suggests that the Lord is anxious for us to receive the blessings. Sometimes we are less than anxious to qualify for them, but according to President Smith, it matters to the Lord that his blessings be received.

One woman's life, which seemed at one time to have no joy, still gives evidence of Heavenly Father's caring a great deal. She told her own story: "Turned out of my home when only a teenager, I made friends with the streetwise girls who introduced me to what must have been all of New York City's places of iniquity. I knew them well. Eventually, however, a boy I had known and loved from my childhood came into my life once again. We married and had nine children. Then, tragically, he was killed in an auto accident and I had no means to care for my family. Bad turned to worse and I turned to alcohol. The state took my children. A friend gave me shelter in an attic, where I lived for seven years, years I scarcely remember for the daze of the drinking.

"One day I said to myself, 'There has to be more to life than this.'

"I offered a simple prayer, saying, 'Please, God, send someone to help me. I can't go to anyone, because I don't know where to go or where to begin.'

"Shortly after that prayer, I was there in my attic room, and I needed a pan to cook with. Because of so little space, my pans hung outside my door. I reached for one and was startled by seeing two young men dressed in dark suits, white shirts, and ties standing there. I cried out in alarm. They calmed my fears by explaining they were missionaries from The Church of Jesus Christ of Latter-day Saints, with a message that would bring great blessings into my life.

"I knew the Lord had sent them. Listening to their message was easy; belief was immediate. From that point, I came from outer darkness into the light and have since been filled with peace and happiness."

She now enjoys full activity in the Church, including temple attendance and service in the Relief Society. Her prayer is that her children, all grown, will come to know the truths that have brought so much joy to her, and this is beginning to happen.

What Elder Joseph Fielding Smith said can help us understand how this woman could recognize the truth when she heard it on the stairs that day. He said: "We lived in the presence of

God in the spirit before we came here. We desired to be like Him, we saw Him, we were in His presence. There is not a soul in this building today who has not seen both the Father and the Son, and in the spirit world we were in their presence."[3]

Speaking of this same truth, President George Albert Smith said: "I wonder sometimes as I travel throughout the country and see the hundreds of thousands of people scattered everywhere, how many of them there are that realize that they are the children of the Lord. He is the Father of our spirits."[4]

Because so many do not know him, finding and teaching these people is one of the major ways we can help the Lord's cause. Doing this demonstrates a love for them and for him. It is also one of the surest ways to strengthen our own faith.

Such love and faith can be readily seen in a letter from a sister missionary. In her desire to reach others with the truth, she indelibly etched it in her own heart. Addressing her extended family in their newsletter, she wrote: "If you cannot think of anyone with whom you can share the gospel, and you truly have the desire to serve in this work, . . . get down on your knees as a family tonight and prayerfully ask the Lord to bring someone into your life who you will be able to help. . . . [Look] for every opportunity to find the lost sheep the Lord would have you shepherd. . . . Invite great joy and blessings into your home and into the lives of those of our brothers and sisters who so desperately need to hear his great message. . . . I know it is true. He lives. My love and prayers. Always, Andrea."

Another young woman who was concerned for the well-being of others noticed among her friends someone she thought could appreciate the truths of the gospel. Through their association she had observed his genuine nature and was quite sincere when, one time as they were talking, she said, "You know, you should be a Mormon bishop." Although he knew many Latter-day Saints (this girl among them), his family was clearly non-Mormon. But he did think about what she said, and wondered what it might mean to him, and he asked a few questions about the Church when it was convenient.

These were the after-high-school years. He was exploring different career options but couldn't seem to settle on one. Finally, after several months of indecision, he thought that perhaps what he needed to do right now was to find out more about the Mormon church. He went to a temple visitors' center and asked if there might be someone who could tell him about the Church. There was. He did join the Church. Later, as a successful missionary, he had a particular understanding for young people who were looking for the truth.

Referring to this great message—the truths of the gospel and particularly of the resurrection and the assurance it brings—Elder Stephen L Richards wrote, in a *Relief Society Magazine* article published in wartime:

> The inestimable blessing of the resurrection inures to all. Every man, woman, and child who has lived or who will live is the beneficiary. . . . It is universal. . . .
>
> How sorely the world needs today the blessings which come from these eternal Gospel truths. . . . Every week, for how long a time nobody knows, will bring more widows, more orphans, more bereaved mothers and fathers, and sad sweethearts. This is the awful penalty of war. It always has been and it always will be.
>
> If a great grief comes to your home, you will need help. Nothing is more precious than one's own flesh and blood, and the loss of a manly son, a devoted husband, or father, or a life mate-to-be is not easily requited. Kinspeople, good friends, and neighbors may come to bring you sympathy, love, and kindness. This will help, but it will not be enough. You will tell yourself that he died in a great cause—in the service of his country. You will convince yourself that it was a noble sacrifice. You will be proud of him, but your heart will still ache and you will have an irrepressible longing once more to see his face, to hear his voice, and have his arms around you and feel again the warmth and tenderness of his loving embrace. Surely you will need help.
>
> I know of one source only from which that help may be secured. It is from this selfsame Jesus who gave His life for others and, on the third day, took it up again. Even with His help you will still weep, but you will not weep in vain. If you will let Him, He

will take away all bitterness from your loss. He will touch your broken heart and it will mend, not all at once, perhaps, but gradually and surely. If you will listen to the voice of His Spirit and His holy Word, He will convince you that your loved one is not lost but only separated from you for a time, and that you may confidently look forward to a happy companionship in the not-too-distant future where there will be no more war, no more cruelty, and no more sad partings from those we love.

It is true that it is necessary that you make preparation for such a glad reunion, but you will know, if you listen to Him, what you are to do, and you will have the joyful assurance that His promises do not fail. This is the comfort and the hope that all of us so sorely need in the days of trial here and ahead. This is the comfort which the One who knew sorrow better than any other left with His disciples to heal their grieving hearts and the broken hearts of all who should come after them.[5]

Prayer is the access to this heavenly help. President J. Reuben Clark, Jr., said: "We seek our Heavenly Father through prayer. It seems that when the Lord was on the earth, he never approached a great event or a seeming crisis in his earth-life, without first going to his Father in prayer."[6]

Sometimes the greatest measure of the power of prayer to comfort and sustain is when answers do not come readily or in the manner hoped for. This was demonstrated by the Christmas card sent by one young family. Even as it sat in the basket with the other cards, this card seemed somehow to stand out. Cheery green paper framed the picture of a smiling, happy family—a young couple with two little boys. The printed words assured the reader not only of their happiness but also of their great love for one another.

The happiness and love radiated to those who received the card. Many knew those smiles could have been tears. The young father, hospitalized for months, now becoming years, was suffering severe symptoms resulting from an infection that left him helpless to speak freely, to walk, to sit up alone, or even to roll over in bed without help. His young wife remained optimistic and courageous despite the unusually heavy demands upon her. Her days included attending the university to complete her schooling, creating a home that radiated joy for their two little boys, and spending sufficient hours with her husband to keep him encouraged and striving for recovery.

Although prayers had been ample and ardent, major difficulties for this little family remained. But the young mother knew the prayers were heard and she continued to believe. The smiles on the Christmas card photo were there in spite of anguish. The family was sustained by a trust in the Lord, a trust already rewarded in the love and happiness they wrote of in their greeting.

Having faith in the principle of prayer and having faith in the Father to whom prayers are addressed may sometimes be easier than to believe in what is in the prayer itself. One account offers help. In 3 Nephi 19:24 we are told that after Jesus had gone apart by himself and prayed to the Father, he came to his disciples, and, it is written, "they did still continue, without ceasing, to pray unto him; and they did not multiply many words, for it was given unto them what they should pray."

When "what to pray" is given by the Spirit, how much easier it is to have effectual faith in that prayer! It erases the doubt that sometimes gets in the way of unwavering faith. Praying when led or prompted by the Spirit teaches us not only what to pray for but also when to pray. Problems as large as those faced by the young family on the Christmas card surely demand the immediate focus of prayer. But prayer can also help in smaller, more daily matters.

Wanting always to serve and please the Lord can lead to many instances when one's own strength or ability is not enough. This was true one evening when a mother sat with her daughter listening to her husband give a speech. It was an often-repeated occasion with these two, for her husband was frequently called upon to speak. This speech, however, was not coming together as well as his talks usually did.

When this became evident to the daughter, she leaned over and whispered to her mother, "Daddy's talk isn't going very well, is it?"

The mother had already felt this and was silently following a prompting to pray. She whispered into the young girl's ear, "Pray for him."

The talk turned out very well for the father that night, and for the mother and daughter, the evening was particularly memorable because of the Spirit and promptings and prayer.

Elder Marion G. Romney gave forceful instruction that applies to listening to spiritual promptings: "My final counsel to you this morning is to learn to recognize and follow the guidance of the Holy Spirit. Without such guidance, even a knowledge of the word of God is unfruitful."[7] Referring to Moroni 10:4–5, he emphasized the latter half of the promise, "And by the power of the Holy Ghost ye may know the truth of all things."

Elder Romney said further:

> The Prophet Joseph seems to have felt that the gift of the Holy Ghost was the most distinguishing characteristic of The Church of Jesus Christ of Latter-day Saints. In 1839, he, with Elias Higbee, went to Washington, D.C. to seek redress from the Government for the wrongs suffered by the saints in Missouri. Writing back to Nauvoo, they said: "In our interview with the President [he is talking about Van Buren, the President of the United States], he interrogated us wherein we differed in our religion from the other religions of the day. Brother Joseph said we differed in mode of baptism, and the gift of the Holy Ghost by the laying on of hands. We considered that all other considerations were contained in the gift of the Holy Ghost."[8]

It is significant for every member of the Church who is serious about living the gospel to know that the Prophet Joseph considered the Holy Ghost to be of that order of importance. Elder Romney counseled that the companionship and guidance of the Holy Ghost merit a conscious and continuing pursuit. But lest we look for the Spirit where it is not, he added the following reminder:

> As we contemplate the virtue of these gifts and fruits [of the Holy Spirit], let me, by the way of caution, emphasize the fact that

there is nothing spectacular, magical, or fanatical about the working of these gifts. Under their influence one behaves perfectly normally. They do not excite. They calm and comfort. Their influence is as natural and refreshing as a gentle breeze. . . .

The following lines of Parley P. Pratt suggest to my mind at least what I'm trying to convey to you concerning the nature and influence of the Holy Spirit.

As the dew from heaven distilling
Gently on the grass descends
And revives it. . . .[9]

One sister testified to this power to revive as she recalled a day when it restored her. She was in the early months of her first pregnancy and on this particular morning was feeling more than a little disconsolate. She was trying not to mind the nausea. She and her husband had wanted this baby a very long time. But the nausea was there, and she was also having some particular anxiety about an unusual pain. And to add to the general discomfort, she was lonely, since they were far away from family and even any close friends.

At the sound of a knock she struggled to her feet. At the door she found a lovely Hawaiian sister who was delivering a cake. This woman was providing for her college student children by selling her excellent baked goods.

The young wife knew the coconut cake would be delicious because she and her husband had bought one before, and she liked the lady, too, so she tried to manage a smile as she paid her. Polynesian people often seem to have a special closeness to the Spirit, and this Hawaiian woman did. She sensed a need, and instead of just saying good-bye, to the younger sister, she said, "Just a minute."

In moments she was back with her ukulele. She sat down on the floor and, forgetting about time, played and sang the beautiful songs of the Islands. The worries of the morning soon paled as the young sister was revived by the sweet spirit this kind woman brought into her home. In subsequent years, the memory of that morning has many times served to inspire pleasant feelings.

Elder Romney concluded: "The Lord has said, 'the Spirit shall be given unto you by the prayer of faith . . .' (D&C 42:14). . . . Develop a desire for it. Live worthy of it and cultivate its companionship. Take it for your guide. If you do so, your rewards will be eternal."[10]

3

GOD HATH SPOKEN

Within these covers, the voice rings out, "God hath spoken."
—*Matthew Cowley*

$\mathcal{S}$hould we ever wonder where attention to the scriptures fits in our priorities, we can remember that when the Lord established his Church in the latter days, he had the Book of Mormon prepared before the formal organization of the Church took place. The Relief Society also had a scriptural foundation. In one of the earliest Relief Society meetings, Joseph Smith instructed the women that the "grand keywords" to guide the society were those Jesus spoke, "Ye shall do the work, which ye see me do."[1] This gave the sisters direction for the service they would perform, but it also implied their study of the scriptures. It was important to them to know well what work the Savior did, so that they could follow his example.

In a 1978 women's fireside address, President Spencer W. Kimball underscored the importance of scripture study for women when he stated, "We want our sisters as well as our men to be scholars of the scriptures."[2] Appropriately, the brethren have often focused their teachings on the standard works when giving instruction to the Relief Society. President George Albert

Smith spoke about the validity of the Lord's word: "The Lord in his mercy began in the very beginning to give the people advice, his advice. He was not guessing about it because he knew. Sometimes we give advice and I fear we just guess about it. . . . How foolish we are, then, not to pay attention to him who is the Father of us all and who loves us . . . , and how foolish we are if we listen to . . . those who are not of God and who do not know what he knows."[3]

This description is reminiscent of the experience of one four-year-old girl on her first trip to the ocean. Having just come from visiting a large amusement park where parental caution and restraints were essential, she saw the open sea and the sand before her as one expansive playground. Dressed in her new pink swimsuit and equipped with her matching pink boogie board, she bounded toward the water, declaring, in all the independence her four years could command, "Now *I'm* in charge!"

Her daddy took her hand, and although he would protect her, he was himself unfamiliar with the power of the ocean's surge. At the breaking of the first good-sized wave she was tumbled and tossed in the churning water. She ran back to her mother, all salty-eyed and sputtering. In a few minutes she courageously tried again, but once more she was dashed by the waves. With a four-year-old's resilience, she quickly turned to building sand castles, and so found a different delight in her day and a good use for her new pink outfit.

But one day she will need to learn that finding joy in the surf comes in recognizing that it is in charge. As she grows wiser, she will know to let the ocean's force lift and carry her, and that her mastery lies in developing skills to work *with* the power of the sea.

Perhaps by the time she has learned more about the sea, she will also have come to know more about the Lord, who created it. She will know that he also "created the heavens and the earth, and all things that in them are" (3 Nephi 9:15) and that while he is Master over all, the thing he wants her to know most about him is that he loves her and wants her safety. In an expression of his love and in order to promote her well-being—and that of us all—

he has given the scriptures, written guidelines for passage through earth life. As President Smith said, he knows; he isn't guessing.

Reading the scriptures—"his advice," as President Smith called them—brings a sense of the Lord's regard for all people. But the scriptures can be very personal as well. Sometimes one particular passage will contain a special message that we feel he intends for us at that moment. Clearly, a spiritual power pervades the scriptures and communicates to the listening reader.

At a 1933 Relief Society conference, Elder Joseph Fielding Smith had more to say about the value of personal scripture study. Referring specifically to the Doctrine and Covenants, he said: "Of course it is not my place to dictate to you and tell you what to do, but it is my place to warn the people and tell them that the Lord has commanded them to search these things. . . . It is a wonderful study, and there is not anything in all this world more pleasing, more delightful or that brings greater joy, not anything."[4] Scripture study can indeed be a source of many great blessings.

One sister's experience provided an unusual example of such blessings. A convert to the Church, this sister was anxious to receive her patriarchal blessing. Although English was a second language for her, her blessing was given by an English-speaking patriarch. As he placed his hands on her head, she felt the Spirit of the Lord. She felt that it was the Lord himself who gave the promises and the counsel through the patriarch. She cherished her copy of the blessing and read it often, even though the biblical-style language made it difficult for her to fully grasp all the meaning.

The experience of receiving her blessing motivated this sister, giving her added impetus to live worthy of the Lord's promises. She undertook scripture reading—in English—as a way to grow in gospel awareness. Once again she labored with the language, but through prayer and diligence it grew easier. The more she read, the more familiar it became.

Then an unexpected and remarkable thing began to happen. As she learned the language of the scriptures and they became more understandable to her, so did her patriarchal blessing. Studying the scriptures not only brought her a clearer understanding of the gospel; it gave her the language skill she needed to more fully comprehend the wording of her blessing.

While not all of us are faced with a language difference as great as this sister had, we can learn, as she did, to become familiar with the language of the scriptures. Then we will better recognize and understand the Lord's direction.

At the October 1960 Relief Society conference, President Joseph Fielding Smith read from the 19th Psalm, which tells many of the benefits that can be gained from reading the scriptures: "The law of the Lord is perfect, converting the soul: the testimony of the Lord is sure, making wise the simple. The statutes of the Lord are right, rejoicing the heart: the commandment of the Lord is pure, enlightening the eyes." (Psalm 19:7–8.) President Smith went on to say:

> Now when this psalm was written, there was no Bible. The Israelites had copies of the Five Books of Moses, and they had some few other writings, but they were not distributed generally. They were in manuscript form and mostly in the hands of the priests.
>
> The members of the Church were not fortunate enough to have copies of the scriptures in their possession. . . . They were taught to be humble . . . , to pray, to worship properly, but they did not have the opportunity to sit down at their tent doors or their porches and pick up the scriptures and read them. . . .
>
> . . . I can understand how they so frequently became careless and indifferent and forgot the commandments of the Lord.[5]

President Smith then talked of how different it is for members of the Church now, with the scriptures widely available to be read in their homes. He asked whether they are being valued and actually studied. Once again he read from the psalm, "More to be desired are they [the scriptures] than gold, yea, than much fine gold: sweeter also than honey and the honeycomb" (Psalm 19:10), and added, "Are they sweet to us like that? . . . When you go into the homes to visit, . . . encourage the mothers to teach their children, to read the scriptures to them."[6]

One mother whose family read the scriptures regularly told of an experience that to her was sweeter than honey and more valued than fine gold. She and her husband and their three young children managed to read the Book of Mormon each morning in spite of pressing schedules. One particular Sunday, however, they read in the evening instead, providing them with a luxury of time they did not have on weekdays.

As one son took his turn reading, a passage raised a question in his mind. In the relaxed setting, he felt free to ask about it. This prompted a discussion that satisfied his concern. Then another son said, "If we are having time for questions, three days ago we read about Christ appearing to the Nephites, and he showed them the prints of the nails in his hands. This happened after he was resurrected, so when are resurrected bodies made perfect?"

In the closeness of their family circle, and through the thoughtful questions of her young sons, the mother recognized that their reading of the scriptures was much more than a duty. By being attentive and observant, by pondering the meaning of the words, the children were coming to a knowledge of the truth. The Lord has said, "I will put my laws into their mind, and write them in their hearts: and I will be to them a God, and they shall be to me a people" (Hebrews 8:10). This was beginning to happen for her children, and certainly it was more to be desired than fine gold.

Not only is it now possible to have copies of the scriptures available to read in most homes, but many people have chosen to display favorite passages in places about the house where they can have an even more immediate presence in the lives of family members. They are often decorative pieces lettered in calligraphy, stitched by hand, burned in wood, or tooled in leather.

A quick survey of such displayed passages generated an interesting list: In the kitchen on a plaque sent from a missionary son, "We do not doubt our mothers knew it" (Alma 56:48); standing next to the framed receipt of the first tithing ever paid (as newlyweds) by the grandparents, "Choose you this day whom ye will serve; . . . but as for me and my house, we will serve the Lord"

(Joshua 24:15); hanging on a wall with family remembrances, "We lived after the manner of happiness" (2 Nephi 5:27).

Additional examples were found: On the wall of a bedroom shared by two brothers, "What manner of men ought ye to be?" (3 Nephi 27:27); on a wall at the foot of the stairs, "Be thou an example of the believers" (1 Timothy 4:12); in a hallway, "My heart is brim with joy" (Alma 26:11); and on a chest in a family room, "If I take the wings of the morning, and dwell in the uttermost parts of the sea; even there shall thy hand lead me, and thy right hand shall hold me" (Psalm 139:9–10).

Scriptural passages made familiar by repetition come to mind quickly to strengthen and stay us in moments of stress, temptation, or trial. They can help to form a bulwark of defense against the world.

In a 1964 Relief Society conference address, Elder Marion G. Romney told the sisters how important it is to use the scriptures and to learn to apply them to situations confronted in day-to-day living. He pointed out that this is the message of Lehi's dream of the tree of life, as recorded in 1 Nephi 8:19–32. Lehi tells of a straight and narrow path leading to the tree of life and of a rod of iron parallel to the path. "Numerous concourses of people" are crowding to reach the tree but fail to follow the path and do not grasp the rod (which represents the word of God). Mists of darkness arise, obscuring the way for many. Some are drowned. Others wander off in strange roads and are lost.

Elder Romney then said:

> We are now at sea in a mist of darkness for the very same reason as were our counterparts in Lehi's vision—namely, because we refuse, as did they, to take advantage of the available means of escape.
>
> The bewildered people of Lehi's dream did not need to be lost. . . . [There] was a straight and narrow path paralleled by an iron rod, leading to the tree of life. The wanderers were in trouble because . . . . [t]hey would not grasp the iron rod and follow the path. . . .
>
> The same thing is true of us modern wanderers. There is no necessity for our bewilderment. The same ample means of escape which were available to them of Lehi's vision, are available to us. . . .

. . . [But God's] word will not save us any more than it saved the wanderers of Lehi's vision unless we make use of it. The fact that we have it is not enough.[7]

Making use of his word begins with reading, thinking about, and becoming familiar with the books of scripture we call the standard works. One young man's use of the Book of Mormon brought positive benefits he had not calculated. Scripture reading had been a daily practice in his home as he was growing up. Now each day on his way to work, his train ride into the city gave him a significant amount of time for worthwhile scripture study.

As he sat down next to a window one morning, a man sat next to him. They exchanged a greeting, and then the young man started to read. The next day the same man sat beside him, and again they spoke, and the young man got out his book to read. The next day the same thing happened, and the next.

This became a pattern for these two. Such a thing not uncommon with commuters. The same people ride each day and often sit in the same places. However, this man sat next to the young reader because by now he too was interested in the book.

It was not until some time later, though, that the man really learned what the book was. Missionaries knocked at his door one day and told him about a book they would like to leave with him. Examining it, he recognized it as the book he had been reading over the shoulder of the young man on the train. The missionaries were understandably surprised when the man said that he already knew this book. Indeed, he was reading it every day and was by now into Alma.

Only later did the young reader learn that his reading had been the means of introducing this man to the Book of Mormon and thereby to the Church. It pleased him that his program of reading had turned out to be more useful even than he had planned.

President George Albert Smith spoke about the advantages of the Lord's teachings. He said they are given "not to prevent us from happiness, but to add to our joy and our comfort and our satisfaction, day by day. . . . That is what these books are for. That is why the Lord gives us so much information that we refer to as scripture. It is not that we may have food and clothing and houses and lands here. That is only a part of it. It is that day by day we may so adjust our lives that we will become more perfect as the years go by."[8]

President Smith also said: "The Lord has given to us the opportunity to go forward, . . . under the influence of the same spirit, if we will, that will be here when our Heavenly Father and Jesus Christ, our Lord, will be here in person."[9]

One sister felt that spirit in a most meaningful way in a time of need. She and her husband were serving a mission many thousands of miles away from their home. One day they received disturbing news. Their daughter, a young wife, mother of three small children and expecting another child, was having complications with her pregnancy. The doctor warned that both her life and the life of the infant were at risk. He told her to prepare a plan for a possible emergency. If it occurred, there would not be time to wonder what to do. The daughter's husband commuted to work each day to another city, adding additional concern that he might be far away at a critical moment.

All of this was alarming to the sister and her husband, who were just leaving for a missionary district meeting some hours away. Although they fasted, their prayers brought the sister no peace; she continued to be fearful for her daughter.

In the motel room that night, after her husband was well asleep, she slipped out of the bed and onto her knees. Though she prayed long, fear dominated her feelings; the Spirit of the Lord did not come. The room was dark and unfamiliar, but she remembered where she had laid her Book of Mormon on the bedside table, and reached for it. She was not able to read in the darkness, but she had always found the peace of the Lord in this book, and so she just held it clasped in her arms, close to her heart. As she did, she seemed to be engulfed by the Lord's Spirit. The fear left and peace filled her soul.

Now when she sees their daughter with her young child, she

remembers a small country town so many thousands of miles away, and the book and the dark night and the goodness of the Lord.

Elder Matthew Cowley told the sisters of his faith in the book: "I know very little about the outside evidences of The Book of Mormon, but I have a testimony of the divinity of this book, and that testimony has come to me from within the two covers of the book itself."[10]

In 1927 President Anthony W. Ivins gave the sisters an extensive discourse on the Book of Mormon. The few excerpts contained here suggest the nature of his address. Its value rests not only in the scope of its doctrine but also in the implication that the sisters of the Church had interests beyond their household responsibilities.

Speaking of the Book of Mormon, President Ivins said:

> We see in it the fulfilment of the words of the prophets uttered hundreds of years ago, for they referred to it in detail, giving the manner of its coming forth, its reception by the world. That which the book would be expected to accomplish was told in detail by Isaiah, by Jeremiah, and others of the ancient prophets. So that if such a book has not come forth or if it has and does not contain the fulness of the everlasting gospel, or if it is not the book which was to be written for Ephraim and the people of Israel, his companions—then we must look forward to the coming forth of some other book because the unchanging decree of the Lord was that such a book should come forth, that it should come out of the earth.

President Ivins continued describing the prophetic anticipation of the book, and then talked of young Joseph Smith's visit from the angel Moroni, commenting:

> It was a very remarkable thing to say of this boy who was almost entirely unknown, scarcely known even to his neighbors, to say that his name would be known throughout all the world. . . .
>
> One of the marvelous things—one of the wonders, is that the following year this book had been translated, prepared for the

printer, and was published to the world. A like achievement I feel certain cannot be found in the world. This is a book of more than five hundred pages. It is a book which treats of the past, the present and the future. . . . And it was all done in a year. It takes time to write books, and particularly books of this kind where the writer makes so many definite declarations of facts.[11]

Elder Marion G. Romney reminded the sisters: "We are today blessed with the word of God in rich abundance. In the Old Testament we have what Lehi's people had in the Brass Plates. In addition, we have the New Testament, The Book of Mormon, the Pearl of Great Price, and the revelations in the Doctrine and Covenants. We also have the teachings of the modern prophets, from the Prophet Joseph Smith to [the present prophet]. The truth in these scriptures would, if followed, lead us into the way of life."[12]

Many specific blessings come to us through the scriptures. They bring peace and comfort in the face of anxiety, understanding to augment learning, direction when uncertainty confuses. However, such a list of blessings is not one that can be checked off and finished, for it grows, and we recognize the eternal nature of the Lord's word, having no end. As he said to Moses, "My works are without end, and also my words, for they never cease" (Moses 1:4).

Although we may not be able to list all the ways we are blessed through the scriptures, the inclusive idea of protection describes a general function they provide. As President Joseph Fielding Smith said: "We have security, the security of the protection of our Father in heaven and his Son Jesus Christ, but that protection is based on our faithfulness in the keeping of his commandments. . . . There never was security in any other way. . . . It is the duty of our sisters, as well as it is of our brethren, to search the scriptures, to become familiar with the things the Lord has revealed. The promises he has made, the covenants he has offered to us, and to walk with understanding and in faith."[13]

4

LIVING THE TRUTH

We ought to live the truth, . . . the truth of the gospel of Jesus Christ.

—*Joseph Fielding Smith*

*F*rom the early days of Relief Society the sisters were encouraged to be holy women—not only to know the Lord's plan but to follow it. Obedience adds both utility and serenity to a woman's life. As Brother Hugh B. Brown said: "Obedience is as necessary as the plan itself. Obedience is evidence of acceptance, and no plan, however perfect, is fully effective unless accepted and worked."[1]

While we may think of obedience as mostly corrective and even with an edge of guilt, sometimes looking positively at what has been accomplished through holding to the commandments helps us to see the power that obedience can engage and how well worth our effort it is.

President George Albert Smith pointed out that such things as favorable living conditions, advancements in science, and growth in the Church are all evidence that someone is meeting the requirements. He said: "Now, all the blessings that have come to us, brothers and sisters, are the result of keeping the commandments of God. All these blessings are not the result of our

willfulness, our carelessness, our indifference, but they are the result of honoring God and keeping his commandments, and there
have been enough of our people who have saved the day for the
rest."[2]

He then referred to the biblical account of the destruction of
Sodom and Gomorrah and Abraham's plea that the righteous not
be destroyed. Abraham was told that the cities would be saved if
ten righteous people could be found.

President Smith continued: "That is how precious righteous
people are. Let us not forget that. If there had been ten righteous
people in those two great cities, and they were populous cities,
the fire would not have come down from heaven to destroy
them, but they would have had another chance."[3]

If we were to look about for righteous people, some that
would seem to qualify are a sister and her family who, despite the
fact that they live near the poverty level, actively seek for persons
who are in need and with whom they can share what little they
have. The stake Relief Society president learned of this when the
sister asked for some extra sheets and blankets. The Relief
Society president thought these were for the woman's own family. But the woman asked the president, "Would you like to see
what I plan to do with these?"

The interested president was then taken to a long-neglected
little dwelling the color of the sand that had blown against it until
the boards were quite bare of paint. Inside, a bed with no bedding, an unsteady table, and a chair were the only furniture. A
family, grouped where they could be together, sat on and about
the bed. They obviously had little more than one another for financial and emotional support. Whether from exhaustion or
hunger, they were listless.

The woman who had asked for the bedding now brought it in
along with some items of clothing and food from her home. After
making the family comfortable for the night, and receiving their
tearful thanks, the woman and the Relief Society president left.

On their way home the Relief Society president learned that
this woman had asked the police department to call whenever

there was a family she could help. Before taking food or clothing from her home, she always told her children something of the problem and asked them if they wanted to help. They always wanted to give something or help in some way.

The two women arrived at the home of the stake Relief Society president, and in the smiles they exchanged as they parted, the women felt a bond of charity and love. They had done what both knew was obedient to the Lord's command, "Feed my sheep" (see John 21:15–17).

"It is impossible for God-fearing women to have anything but noble faces," said President Heber J. Grant. "The face is an index to the character."[4] Further, for developing character there is no substitute for obedience, for doing the right. President Grant believed this strongly and bore witness to it often.

Heber J. Grant's life spanned the years from settlement to city in the Salt Lake Valley. His mother was a widow and he was her only child. She was the ward Relief Society president, so he spent much of his boyhood playing at her feet as she met with other women. He told of a close acquaintance with the early Relief Society leaders, but especially with "Aunt Eliza," as he called Eliza R. Snow.

He often said that apart from his mother, Aunt Eliza had the greatest influence on him in those impressionable years. Young Heber treasured her every account of the Prophet Joseph Smith. Through her vivid recollections he came to know Joseph's character and teachings, his trials and accomplishments. He grew to love the Prophet and the gospel for which Joseph gave his life. Motivated by that love, President Grant lived his own life in energetically furthering the gospel cause. He said:

> The principal task of my life has been to encourage people to do things—to keep the Word of Wisdom, to pay tithing, to teach the children, and to attend to family prayers. I am not a preacher on theory of the gospel, but I have tried to encourage people to do their duty. There is one thing that has been born and bred in me; that is the teaching of obedience, by my mother.

If there is one thing more than another that I would like to do, with the ability which God has given me, it is to impress upon the hearts of the Latter-day Saints to keep the commandments of the Lord; to serve God with full purpose of heart. By so doing I can promise that you will grow in grace in the sight of God, and in the light, knowledge, and testimony of this great Latter-day work. . . .

. . . We have that which will take us back into the presence of God.[5]

Although President Grant was, as he said, "not a preacher on theory of the gospel," Elder (later President) Joseph Fielding Smith was. He was known throughout the Church for his study of and preaching about gospel doctrine. For years he responded in the Church magazines to questions readers submitted. His published books have also been considered a valuable reference.

The scriptures teach that "in the mouth of two or three witnesses shall every word be established" (2 Corinthians 13:1). The next excerpt is an example of a second witness that helps to establish the first. Speaking of obedience, Elder Joseph Fielding Smith made much the same plea as President Grant, only in a different manner. Notice that each presents the principles and the promises.

It is not possible, as some of us have supposed, for us to slip along easily through this life, keeping the commandments of the Lord indifferently, accepting some of the doctrines and not others and indulging our appetites or desires and because we consider them little things, failing to understand and comprehend our duty in relation to them, and then expect to receive a fulness of glory in the kingdom of God. . . .

. . . If you want to become heirs, . . . and partake of the blessings which our Redeemer partakes of, then you must be willing to receive every word that proceeds from the mouth of our Father in heaven. . . .

. . . Those who receive the fulness will be privileged to view the face of our Father.[6]

Along with their witness of gospel truth, these two prophets and their quite different statements concerning the principle of obedience and its promises provide an example of another truth—that representatives of the Lord are not copies of one another. Each of these brethren accepted the same doctrine, the same practices of obedience, and the same requirements for Church members. Both were undoubtedly beloved of the Father. Yet each was quite different from the other. This realization might help allay the misperception that all those who try to live by the rules of the gospel are just alike. To know each person as an individual is to learn that no two are really the same. Though they may share beliefs and practices, each one has unique characteristics, talents, and ideas to be appreciated. The discerning will find pleasure in noting the individualities.

Elder Melvin J. Ballard gave some thoughtful comment about the same commandments, character, and promises discussed by President Grant and Elder Smith. He gave a useful reminder of a precept set forth memorably in the eleventh chapter of Hebrews. After describing the trials and faith of Noah, Abraham, and Sarah, Paul wrote, "These all died in faith, not having received the promises, but having seen them afar off, and were persuaded of them, and embraced them" (Hebrews 11:13).

Elder Ballard cited the Beatitudes (see Matthew 5:1–11), each with its particular promise, and then said:

> There is one very impressive thing about all these promises. The blessings are not to be immediate, they are to come bye and bye. If we should feel the immediate benefits of our action at once, we might be prompted, just for the reward, to do these things; but to continue to be merciful, continue in the spirit of these instructions for all one's life, and yet not realize the reward will take a sustaining faith that looks into a distant future, even an eternity, to get its reward. . . . Those who must have their returns immediately, at the end of each week, month or season, and who if the returns do not come are ready to abandon the enterprise, are at a low state of civilization, but those who can go on, looking to a distant future to realize the blessings of their struggles and labors, will attain a high state of civilization.[7]

Elder Ballard also spoke of early members of the Church as examples:

> Many of our parents were driven from their own homes, and yet they were sustained by this promise. If you are evilly spoken of for my sake, great shall be your reward, and so while they did not realize in life these blessings, they have gone to their reward. . . . They labored to subdue the desert. Sometimes when we talk of the depression that we seem to feel so keenly, they would scarcely have noticed the struggle through which we are passing, it would have been so slight to them, because they had such serious problems, but they looked to a distant future, they were not going to reap the harvest of their struggles, their children were going to reap them. And so they did attain to a high state of civilization.[8]

President David O. McKay spoke praise for the pioneers, particularly the sisters who, he said, may not have been given as much recognition as they merit:

> You will find few if any of their names inscribed on monuments erected to the brave. Some are not even known beyond their family circles; not a few lie in unmarked graves out on the plains, but the burdens they bore uncomplainingly, the contributions they made to the settlement of the arid West, the virtues they exemplified in the midst of trials and almost super-human endurance entitle them to an honored place among the heroines of the world. . . .
>
> One of the most tragically heroic epochs in Church history, one in which are exemplified the dauntless faith and divine leadership of the men at the head of the Church, and the super-human, sublime patience, and resourcefulness of the women, is the period following the expulsion of the saints from Nauvoo. . . .
>
> It is difficult for us who attempt to pay a feeble tribute to these pioneers . . . even to imagine, for example, what those shelterless mothers endured during the month of February 1846—note the month—as they passed through the throes of confinement on the banks of the Sugar Creek when nine babies were born [one night]. . . . The world will do well to pause and think what it was that inspired the women to endure uncomplainingly such trials. . . .

In that month, women, driven from their comfortable homes in Nauvoo, left their land, which many of them could not sell, . . . taking nothing with which they could do without, [and] crossed the Mississippi River to begin a trackless journey.[9]

In the same talk, President McKay related an account of the Martin Handcart Company. The story has often been retold, but it is always affecting as it describes how the power of heaven reaches a hand to sustain when a need is beyond human strength. President McKay quoted William Palmer, who was present when this incident took place, as follows:

Some sharp criticism of the Church and its leaders was being indulged in for permitting any company of converts to venture across the plains with no more supplies or protection than a handcart caravan afforded.

An old man in the corner sat silent and listened as long as he could stand it, then he arose and said things that no person who heard him will ever forget. His face was white with emotion, yet he spoke calmly, deliberately, but with great earnestness and sincerity.

In substance [he] said, "I ask you to stop this criticism. You are discussing a matter you know nothing about. Cold historic facts mean nothing here, for they give no proper interpretation of the questions involved. Mistake to send the Handcart Company out so late in the season? Yes. But I was in that company and my wife was in it and Sister Nellie Unthank whom you have cited was there, too. We suffered beyond anything you can imagine and many died of exposure and starvation, but did you ever hear a survivor of that company utter a word of criticism? Not one of that company ever apostatized or left the Church, because everyone of us came through with the absolute knowledge that God lives for we became acquainted with him in our extremities.

"I have pulled my handcart when I was so weak and weary from illness and lack of food that I could hardly put one foot ahead of the other. I have looked ahead and seen a patch of sand or a hill slope and I have said, I can go only that far and there I must give up, for I cannot pull the load through it." And a wife with a baby in her arms by his side! "I have gone on to that sand and when I reached it, the cart began pushing me. I have looked back many times to see who was pushing my cart, but my eyes saw no one. I knew then that the angels of God were there.

"Was I sorry that I chose to come by handcart? No. Neither then nor any minute of my life since. The price we paid to become acquainted with God was a privilege to pay, and I am thankful that I was privileged to come in the Martin Handcart Company."[10]

Again, consider President McKay's injunction, "The world will do well to pause and think what it was that inspired the women to endure."[11]

What was their inspiration? An answer to that question was expressed by President J. Reuben Clark, Jr.: "We are proving whether we are worthy to go back into the inner family circle of our heavenly home, whether we can mingle with our Heavenly Father and Mother throughout the eternities to come."[12]

One wonders what can match a handcart for proving worthiness. The perspective of time is needed to put a comparative measure on the problems of today. But for now as in years past, one thing is clear—the proving of worthiness is a daily matter.

Examples of this daily effort are abundant. One is the woman who said good-bye to husband and son as they boarded a twin-engine plane for a four-hour trip, only to learn later that her husband had been killed when the plane crashed. The next Sunday the woman bore testimony that although her husband was gone, she would continue to do her part. She would pay the mortgage, send her son on a mission, and help the other children through school with what she could earn. She was certain the Lord would sustain her.

Another sister, a nurse, along with her physician husband, was serving a medical mission to a hospital and orphanage in Eastern Europe. Due to medical problems of her own, they were obliged to return home for her treatment.

Because her condition required surgery and time for recovery, and because Christmas was very close, they were offered the opportunity to stay home and spend the holiday with their children and grandchildren. That was attractive, but the thought of the orphans and the hospital patients, and of how they might make this a wonderful Christmas for them, was more compelling. They went back to their mission, knowing that now was their opportunity to serve those people, and, hopefully, there would be other Christmases they could spend with their family.

The thousands of full-time missionaries now serving the Church worldwide are another example of the price paid daily for the gospel's sake. New groups enter the Missionary Training Center each week. Each young Elder and Sister who comes leaves an empty place in a home. While parents are thankful their sons and daughters are worthy and healthy and want to go, home ties are cut only with deep emotion.

One family had a son and a daughter each serving in a remote place. Every day their absence was felt as keenly as the day each stepped on the plane to leave. "But when we think of those who have heard the gospel because of them, the pain becomes a privilege," their mother said. For example, the daughter was able to teach a part-member Tongan family. The Tongan mother, a member, was able to see the father and all their children baptized, making them a complete and possibly eternal family. The parents of the missionaries say they feel that theirs is the opportunity to give up their children for a short while to enable another family to be united forever.

President George Albert Smith said: "Now, think of what we have here. Think of the righteous men and women that live in the community that you live in, and they are righteous. They are not perfect. I do not know any perfect people, but I have known some that it seemed to me were just as near perfect as it was possible to be. That is what the Lord has promised. If you seek first, not last, but seek *first* the kingdom of God and his righteousness and all other things will be added that are worthwhile. That is what he means."[13]

To understand what the Lord means is our hope. We remember the charge to early sisters to be holy women. It is not always comfortable or convenient to put God's kingdom first. It wasn't so for the Savior. But that is the way we will come closest to him. Each of us with our personal set of conditions will need to individually determine those choices that can make us eligible for the blessings of the faithful.

In a 1943 *Relief Society Magazine* article, Elder Joseph Fielding Smith wrote of the Savior's suffering and commented that we cannot fully comprehend that agony. He quoted Doctrine and Covenants 19:16–19, part of which reads: "Which suffering caused myself, even God, the greatest of all, to tremble because of pain, and to bleed at every pore, and to suffer both body and spirit" (D&C 19:18). Then Elder Smith said:

> It is, however, within our grasp to know and realize that this excruciating agony of His sacrifice has brought to us the greatest blessing that could possibly be given. Moreover, we are able to realize that this extreme suffering—which was beyond the power of mortal man either to accomplish or endure—was undertaken because of the great love which the Father and the Son had for mankind. We are extremely ungrateful to our Father and to His beloved Son when . . . we are unwilling to keep the commandments. . . .
>
> . . . If we fully appreciated the many blessings which are ours through the redemption made for us, there is nothing that the Lord could ask of us that we would not anxiously and willingly do. Why cannot we, today, show forth the faith, and thereby gain the happiness, which was had among the Nephites when it was said of them:
>
> . . . they did walk after the commandments which they had received from their Lord and their God, continuing in fasting and prayer, and in meeting together oft both to pray and to hear the word of the Lord. . . .
>
> And it came to pass that there was no contention in the land, because of the love of God which did dwell in the hearts of the people.
>
> . . . and surely there could not be a happier people among all the people who had been created by the hand of God. [4 Nephi 1:12, 15–16.][14]

5

HOME AS A HOLY PLACE

To the Latter-day Saint, the home is a holy place.
—J. Reuben Clark, Jr.

hus Zion's light is bursting forth / To bring her ransomed children home" ("The Morning Breaks," *Hymns,* 1985, no. 1). These words of Parley P. Pratt evoke a sense of the glory manifest in the light and truth of the restored gospel of Jesus Christ breaking forth upon the world. And nowhere does Zion appear more glorious than in the household of a righteous Latter-day Saint family, where there is a vision of home and its importance in the plan of the restored gospel, and where family members recognize that God is the Father of their spirits.

Little children, when they are very young, are taught the words: "I am a child of God / And he has sent me here. / . . . Teach me all that I must do / To live with him someday." (Naomi W. Randall, "I Am a Child of God," *Hymns,* 1985, no 301.) Church members realize they have the responsibility to prepare these children to live in the presence of the Father again. So we see homes where eternal truths become daily doctrine, where tithing is taught as inevitably as the times tables.

No agency has been organized to fill the needs of mankind so well as the home. President David O. McKay said, "Home is based in the very constitution of human nature, and so vital is the relation which it sustains to our needs, that every heart must have a home."[1]

In the early years of this dispensation, new members of the Church recognized the role of the home in relation to spiritual needs. They often gathered to where others shared this understanding, and there they established a home in the security of a common faith. This desire led one family in nineteenth-century England to leave all behind and cross sea, desert, and mountain range until they found that safe place.

James and Ann, his wife, were both in their middle years when they heard and accepted the gospel. In 1855 they were baptized. Because of their "Mormon" faith, they were promptly turned out of the rented house in which they lived. The owner, a minister in the Church of England, told them they could stay if they would give up their belief. James replied, "My religion is a pure and undefiled religion. It is the religion of the Lord Jesus Christ, and I would not give it up for your house or this town or all that my eyes have ever beheld."

They joined a group of Latter-day Saints who were migrating to the valleys of the Rocky Mountains. Drawn by their love of the Lord, these travelers all hoped for a place where they could establish a home. Ann was happy contemplating life in Zion. But she was not physically strong and could not endure the journey. She died and was buried at sea. James made his way to the valley alone, remaining true to the gospel they loved.

Larger groups have moved as a people for much the same reason. Consider the children of Israel going from Egypt to the promised land, the Puritans coming to America, and the Jews gathering from throughout the world to form the modern state of Israel. They, too, felt the imperative of finding a home—felt, as President McKay said, the crucial "relation which it sustains to our needs."

President J. Reuben Clark, Jr., clarified just what "our needs" in relation to home are: "Thus we came from a celestial home to this earth; we shall return to a celestial home when we leave this world. In that home Jesus is our Elder Brother, which shows our dignity, our rights, and our privileges."[2]

As President Clark pointed out, the home our spirits knew before coming to earth was celestial. One father who understood that relationship wanted his children to recognize the eternal bond that links their home and family to Heavenly Father. He planned a Christmas morning experience to help bring them to this awareness. To surprise his wife, he made arrangements with each child before the day arrived. Early Christmas morning each one came to the family room dressed all in white. They each had a gift wrapped in white for their mother. The father then called to the mother, asking her to hurry down to where they were all assembled waiting for her. She came quickly. As she stepped into the room she saw the heavenly scene of all their children dressed in white. The tree lights sparkled, but not as brightly as the light in the eyes of each child. In turn they gave their gifts to their mother, along with their expressions of appreciation to her for making their home a heavenly place.

Never had angels and the light of Christmas seemed closer than they did that day to the surprised and deeply touched mother. Never had her family seemed more dear.

This father had created an experience that would encourage his children to think of their home as a sacred, holy place and that would help them to see how they contributed to that spirit. Having them dress in white reminded them of the divinity in each of them. He then helped them to recognize the extraordinary role of their mother in creating a home suitable for spirit children of Heavenly Father. The lovely feeling generated by the experience has lingered in their home. The children more easily express their love for family members, especially their mother, since their participation that morning.

Knowing about our relationship to the divine gives more purpose to some of our desires and aspirations. It explains that innate something in each of us that reaches for what is higher and better. When directed by the Spirit of the Lord, this impetus can lead us to find, to borrow a scriptural phrase, "a more excellent way" (1 Corinthians 12:31)—as this young father did on Christmas morning.

Two Relief Society sisters in South America, a mother and her daughter, realized a more excellent way as it was taught to them. Converts to the Church, they were eager to implement all they were learning.

A homemaking meeting focused on improving one's surroundings. As they pondered what the lesson could mean to them, they thought of the place where they lived in poverty. The structure itself was less than meager, barely offering protection from the elements. It had no covering for the dirt floor. But their strong desire to improve was a witness of their expanding belief in a better way.

First they found a very large rock that served quite well for a table. Then they found enough string to crochet a doily. On that they placed a shiny can filled with wild flowers they picked. It was a better way! With this final touch, the improvement project was completed. But their personal development had only begun. The experience with their home taught them that through the programs of the Church—and with the Lord's help—their lives could change.

Though they lived in humble circumstances, these sisters provided an example of two important concepts. First, their experience demonstrates that there is a blessing for every person who exercises faith in the programs of the Church and diligently carries them through. The blessings of home are not limited to a certain group. There is no mention in President Clark's comment, for example, that only some of us came from a celestial home. There was no qualification in the homemaking lesson that only sisters with husbands should try to improve their surroundings, or only those who had easy access to furniture, paint, or carpet. These women believed that the lesson had meaning for them. Because they did, it led them to experience a kind of joy that transformed not only their home but their lives.

The second way these sisters served as models for others was in using what they had, meager as it was.

President Heber J. Grant made an emphatic plea to the sisters of the Church to live within their incomes. He believed most difficulties over money could be avoided by observing that one rule. He counseled:

> There is nothing more true than that we have tried to live beyond our means as a people, and any person who does that gets into trouble. . . .
>
> There is a peace and a contentment which comes into the heart when we live within our means. . . .
>
> If there is any one thing that will bring peace and contentment into the human heart, and into the family, it is to live within our means, and if there is any one thing that is grinding, and discouraging and disheartening it is to have debts and obligations that one cannot meet.[3]

President Grant taught that one way to prevent materialism from overshadowing the gospel in our homes is to confine worldly wants to those in keeping with the family's ability to pay.

A practical lesson was learned by one family when they were traveling on a combined business and vacation trip. As the family entered each new city where they planned to spend a night, the children looked for the most elaborate accommodations, those with amusement areas and swimming pools. After several days of what was becoming overspending, the parents decided to explain to the children about their per diem—that they were allowed a certain amount of money for each day's expenses. They invited the children to help keep the family financial record, with each child having certain responsibilities.

The mood of the trip changed entirely. The children were soon finding motels with kitchenettes so the family could prepare some of their own meals. They became so thrifty, in fact, that the parents wondered about some of the places they chose to stay. This led to a discussion about which comforts might be worth added cost. In the end, rather than spending the considerable additional money it at first appeared they might, the family came home well under budget. The children actually had a good time trying their hand at managing the expenses and had a decided sense of achievement at having ended the trip with a positive balance. This approach worked so well that even after returning home, the parents continued to assign some of the family financial responsibilities to the children in what became an ongoing program of conservation.

This practical aspect to creating a home, though mundane, has definite spiritual implications. Financial stresses can affect the spirituality of a home. Although we hope to have our homes centered on heavenly influences, we still must respond appropriately to earthly realities.

Elder Thomas S. Monson called to mind the frequency with which the Savior alluded to home and home building in his parables, which used for topics the very substance from which the peoples' lives were made:

> When the Savior walked the dusty pathways of towns and villages which we now reverently call the Holy Land and taught his disciples by beautiful Galilee, he often spoke in parables, in language the people best understood. Frequently he referred to home building in relationship to the lives of those who listened.
>
> He declared: ". . . every . . . house divided against itself shall not stand" (Matt. 12:25). And then, in this dispensation, cautioned: "Behold, mine house is a house of order, saith the Lord God, and not a house of confusion" (D&C 132:8). At Kirtland he said, "Organize yourselves; prepare every needful thing; and establish a house, even a house of prayer, a house of fasting, a house of faith, a house of learning, a house of glory, a house of order, a house of God" (D&C 88:119).[4]

Searching these teachings of the Savior may give some insights into qualities characterizing the celestial home. "A house divided against itself" suggests that before a home can achieve strength, there needs to be agreement on what a home should be. Agreeing on the goal makes possible a unity of purpose in striving to reach it. This in turn brings stability.

The next teaching of the Lord mentioned by Elder Monson is that found in Section 132 of the Doctrine and Covenants: "Mine house is a house of order." The word *order* is used as the Lord refers to ordinances, exactness, and obedience in keeping the covenants. Although ordinances are to be performed with exactness, and obedience to covenants must be strictly observed, it is in the performance of these very functions that one can often exhibit the greatest manifestations of love.

One thoughtful father who served faithfully as a bishop knew the responsibility of looking to the needs of every member of his ward. He believed that he must pray for wisdom to counsel, understanding to guide, and power to bless each ward member in need of help. As he did these things, he realized that he had just as great a necessity to call forth the Lord's blessing for his own family. He learned that the calling of the bishop, as father of the ward could in fact be a guide to every father for effectively bringing the powers of heaven into his own home.

He knew that his wife, in her special relationship with the children, sought for and received the Lord's inspiration. As their father he also had the obligation for divinely directed service to them. With renewed dedication, he sought the Lord, often in fasting, always in prayer. He looked for each opportunity to use his priesthood power to bless his family. In free moments—even brief periods of time—he pondered the problems of family members. He studied the scriptures regularly for added direction. He found that the Lord often made known to him the basic needs of a child, even needs that were not readily apparent. This allowed him, as a father, to give inspired counsel. Similarly, he was sometimes guided as to promises that could be made and blessings that could be pronounced. The more earnestly he tried to be worthy of the Lord's blessings for his family, the more his understanding grew. So did his gratitude for his priesthood opportunities in his home. He began to realize what "a house of order" can mean.

The next of the teachings Elder Monson referred to was, "Organize yourselves." We need go no further than this to find a quality that could make a major change in some homes. To think of a heavenly home without organization would be akin to finding a unit of the Church without a presiding officer and assigned leaders.

Some homes organize only when a need arises, then fall back into disarray until another cause to mobilize, and so they live from crisis to crisis. But if we follow the Lord's model for organizing our homes, "preparing every needful thing," we can avoid some of the emergencies and be ready to deal with others.

The remainder of this scripture is especially valuable because in the Lord's description of the temple, we can see what should be incorporated into the homes we establish: prayer, fasting, faith, learning, glory, and order; and finally, they should be houses of God. Achieving any of these goals could be considered a triumph. But the effort of continuing until all are obtained will be even more worthwhile, for in that completion will come a wholeness approaching "perfectness and peace" (see D&C 88:125).

Thus, although Doctrine and Covenants 88:119 has special meaning in reference to temples, it seems appropriate to apply this passage also to our own homes. And the idea that one could actually establish "a house of glory, a house of order, a house of God" is humbling to contemplate. The wonder of the Lord's statement is that all of these are included in one list of instructions, implying that it is possible, even anticipated, that this is what our homes can become. The truth is that in having chosen the Lord's way we have become a part of a grand program, an exalted concept of life that is offered to every person who is willing to accept it.

President J. Reuben Clark, Jr., explained further: "Thus in our existence here, we are carrying out the plan which was made for the great celestial family of which we are a part; we are going forward as the children of our God and fitting into the pattern He made for us. The place we shall hold in God's household, in God's family, in our heavenly and eternal home, whether it shall be in the inner family circle, or outside in the halls and anterooms, depends wholly upon what we ourselves do here."[5]

President Clark's description causes us to think freshly about our coming to earth, away from all with which we were accustomed, to see if we would make the same choice here that we did there. The fact that we are here on earth with a mortal body is indication that before we came here we did choose the Lord's plan.

One of the ways we can prepare to be in the family circle of God's household is to establish a home as nearly like his as we can. This may be the very reason the Lord has provided such specific instructions. We do know that qualities approaching the celestial are already a common practice in many homes. We learn from one another through such examples. In the *Lectures on Faith* we are taught that the knowledge of the existence of God is established through the testimony of others.[6] In a somewhat similar way we can learn qualities of godliness as they are exhibited in exemplary family life.

One sister said the assurance of her mother's love was one of the constants in her home life. She could turn to her mother if things did not go well at school or if friends disappointed her. She remembered how her mother always seemed to understand, to find the truth in a difficult situation, and to have the capacity for limitless love.

These memories of her mother came to her mind pointedly when her own daughter pleaded for leniency after a misdeed. It was on a Sunday. The family had come home from an afternoon conference session. The daughter, who had been baptized earlier that very day, suddenly disappeared. She did not come home when called. Though her mother was confident the daughter was playing with a friend, it was unusual that she did not respond and did not come in at supper time. Only when the sun was beginning to set did she return.

Vexed at least as much from worry as from concern for her misbehavior, this sister spent little time with conversation. She sent her daughter right to bed. The child complied, for she recognized her wrongdoing. But as she was going to her room she said, "I would just like to tell you this one thing. Our Primary teacher said the Holy Ghost would tell me all the things I should do. Well, I listened, and listened, and listened and he never *did* tell me it was time to come home."

The sister took her daughter in her arms and explained to her about spiritual feelings.

Another sister related an incident that strengthened her relationship with her father. She was years too young to drive a car, but had persuaded her older sister to let her try just for a short distance. This was in a time and place when people learned to drive by driving, so although her being at the wheel was unwise, it was not unlawful. It was, however, unfortunate. In that short distance she crashed into a telephone pole. Neither she nor her sister was seriously hurt, but the car was severely damaged. Of course she was penitent and terribly frightened. It was the only car the family had, and it would not be easy to get another. When she went with her father to see the wreckage, he looked it over and shook his head a bit. Then, perhaps knowing she could not feel worse than she did already, he said not a word of criticism but walked back with her to the house—a kindness she will never forget.

"There can be no real home life where there is no love," said President J. Reuben Clark, Jr. He also gave some other essential characteristics that any true-hearted home builder will want to consider: "Next, there must be prayer; a prayerless abode is not a home. There must be in that home, honor. . . . There must be seemliness in the home. . . . A vulgar story has no place around the home fire. . . . Bring into your home the best of culture, of education. . . . Make your home life as near heaven life as you can."[7]

Another sister learned to honor the temple by the way her mother cared for her temple clothes. In an attitude of respect the mother cleaned, pressed, folded, packed, and stored. All that she did with her sacred clothing told her daughter that the clothing was to be honored and that attending the temple was a privilege.

"In our sacred temples the blessings of heaven are bestowed upon the truly faithful and from that holy place they may be carried into our individual homes," said Elder Mark E. Petersen. He also declared that homes should be blessed with the power of the priesthood, whether it be through fathers, brothers, bishops, or home teachers. He said: "So let us recognize the priesthood, then, for what it is—the power of God given to us in this mortal life. And let us remember its purpose—to bless and guide and exalt, and to assure every home of God's omnipresence, not only through the power of his Holy Spirit, but likewise through the physical presence of his duly ordained servants."[8]

Through the years, in their counsel to the sisters the brethren have taught of home as an exalted ideal. In their prophetic callings they have urged the women to choose well for their households and build strong defenses against the world. In a 1978 women's fireside address, President Spencer W. Kimball, helping the sisters see that they have a critical role to fill, said to them, "Other institutions in society may falter and even fail, but the righteous woman can help to save the home, which may be the last and only sanctuary some mortals know in the midst of storm and strife."[9] To know how to help we must understand the importance of home for each individual, and that all are included in the eternal plan.

President J. Reuben Clark, Jr., said:

The righteous life is not prescribed by a whimsical or capricious Deity. The prescriptions for such a life have their source deep in the secrets of eternity. They lead men to the highest degrees of glory, to the loftiest pinnacle of celestial achievement.

Latter-day Saints know that these matters are not idle theories, concocted over the ages in the minds of men; they know that these are the basic facts of existence. . . .

One can stand only in awful and reverent silence at the grandness and glory of this vision of our promised destiny, predicated upon the building of a true home.[10]

6

SPIRITUALITY COMES
INTO ITS OWN

Spirituality comes into its own in . . . a family circle.
—Mark E. Petersen

$\mathcal{O}$ne of the universal truths of mankind is the fact that we are all the offspring of parents, a father and a mother. The similarities may end there, for the circumstances under which every infant grows are so varied. Because not all have experienced childhood and youth in what might be called a traditional home, nor has every person been a parent in such a family, each may relate to the concept of family differently.

The following statement of Elder Ezra Taft Benson and the one a bit further on by President J. Reuben Clark, Jr., clearly define the Father's eternal plan regarding families and his way of bringing his spirit children to the earth. There are many other considerations that pertain to individuals. For example, one's present circumstance may not seem to be moving toward that eternal plan, or many do not have the family experience they would envision for themselves. But it is, nonetheless, useful to see a comprehensive statement of what the Lord's plan is, remembering always that it is eternal and we, in mortality, see ourselves in a small fragment called time. Elder Benson said: "The family is a divine institution established by our Heavenly Father. It is basic to civilization and particularly to Christian civilization. The establishment of a home is not only a privilege, but marriage and the bearing, rearing, and proper training of children is a duty of the highest order."[1]

There may be no better way to influence civilization than through a family. The family's power to affect the life of a single individual is suggested in this statement by Feodor Dostoyevsky: "There is nothing higher and stronger and more wholesome and useful for life in later years than some good memory, especially a memory connected with childhood, with home. If a man carries many such memories with him into life, he is safe to the end of his days, and if we have only one good memory left in our hearts, even that may sometime be the means of saving us."[2]

The making of memories sometimes "just happens." But it may happen more often when a conscious effort to bring together memorable circumstances is made. One woman made many occasions memorable for those affected by them. She did it with Church programs for which she was responsible. But she expended special effort to make family gatherings events to be happily remembered. She would frequently ask, "What can we do to make this important to them?" As a consequence, her husband, her children, and those who worked with her knew that her regard for them was such that they always merited her best effort.

President J. Reuben Clark, Jr., placed the family unit in a larger context:

> We come now to our earthly family unit and its place in the universes of God's creations. Here we see there is another purpose for our existence on earth besides so living that we shall go back into the presence of God, to live with him, to take our place at the inner home fireside of the celestial family of our Father. We can now see that just as each mortal family here may be the parent of other mortal families, so God's celestial family is the parent of

other celestial families. Each family unit here, that is created by and under the authority of the priesthood in the House of the Lord, is potentially another celestial family, another Heavenly Home, like to the one of which we are members,—a family unit that may ultimately do for other intelligences what God did for ours, even to the full eternal plan, for the Great Design is God's perfect plan.

But such a destiny for the family unit is predicated upon the observance of very definite laws. . . .

Thus every earthly family unit, that is properly begun by a marriage in a House of the Lord performed by one having authority thereto has within its reach this infinite opportunity of eventually becoming creators after eternities of schooling and preparation; they have the infinite opportunity of heading another celestial family, which means the power and opportunity of creating worlds and peopling them. This is the supreme work, the very highest glory of which God has told us. Even its appreciative contemplation is almost beyond our finite reach.

The Psalmist sang: "I have said, Ye are gods; and all of you are children of the most High." (Ps. 82:6)[3]

When giving this thorough and definitive explanation of the eternal progression of families, President Clark stated: "Even its appreciative contemplation is almost beyond our finite reach." His comment is reminiscent of a little boy who had just heard an explanation given by his father, a professor. The father was accustomed to speaking to his children much as he did the college students he taught. Usually they followed the reasoning. This time, however, the young son felt stretched beyond his four-and-a-half-year-old vocabulary and said, "Daddy, can you simple that down a little?"

His father took the explanation in smaller steps for him, and the boy then could grasp the concept. He went on to more and more complex ideas, to higher learning, until finally, not unlike families generating more families, this young man became a teacher of other students, and also, a father of other young boys.

Going from where we are, with limited understandings, to the infinite possibilities described to us here by President Clark is not beyond our reach. Indeed it is the plan of our Father for each of us. President David O. McKay gave certain sure steps that must be followed: "Parents should be sufficiently companionable with their boys and girls as to merit their children's confidence. They should be companions with them. When parents shirk this duty, perhaps teachers can succeed where parents fail."[4]

It takes time to be a friend to a young person. But even in a world where time seems to be at a premium, becoming a positive part of a young person's life can be considered a good investment. One great-grandmother, talking to a granddaughter sponging down the fevers of two small boys with measles, reflected on her life of nearly eighty years. She spoke of rearing nine children in a time when water for washing clothes was heated in a large tub over a fire. There had been many anxieties because medical care was not readily available. It had been hard to have the time to do all that was needed for each child, even though she had tried.

Then she said: "I shouldn't have thought it a hardship though, because now with the passing years the difficulties pale, and the children are the great joy of my life."

One extended family understands the value of time spent to-gether in strengthening family bonds and each individual's sense of belonging. They spend a long weekend in a place apart from their usual contacts. They focus on being together. They stage their own "Summer Olympics," games where all cheer for those who race against their own best time. Spectators receive as many medals as participants. With emphasis on sharing rather than competing, love grows with every event. Appreciation also builds with each meal prepared by assigned teams of family members!

One example offers a measure of how effective their time to-gether is. After a day of cheering on brothers and cousins, one little three-year-old girl awakened her parents in the night with the cry, "Come on, Stephen. You can do it!" She was dreaming about her brother's race. In such a happy atmosphere of cheering one another on, there is no difficulty in making the "Olympics" an annual occurrence.

President Stephen L Richards appealed to the sisters to

recognize the privilege of teaching, training, and loving the spirit children of Heavenly Father. All children are first and always his, born in the spirit as children of that Father. Ours is the sacred opportunity to give them earthly bodies, and more important, to care for them and teach them to live so as to return to him. President Richards made a strong statement that offers a solution to the ills of the world, including those in our own homes:

> Would that all men could be brought to an acute realization . . . that some day the spirits of those who have been the victims of tyranny, oppression, and even neglect, will arise to accuse their oppressors, and that the God of justice will impose the penalty.
>
> My sisters, you may think that this revealed principle, demanding respect and justice for the spirit children of our Father tabernacled in the bodies of men, applies chiefly, if not entirely, to the tyrants and oppressors of the race throughout the world. It goes much further. It has application in all our living, and particularly in relation to the family. I know of no more salutary principle in all our theology than that a home is a religious institution, into which the Father permits his spirit children to come and abide in mortal tabernacles, and that the mission, the predominant, transcendent mission of parenthood is to bring the spirit children entrusted to their care back into the presence of the Father. . . . I have no hesitancy in making the declaration that if that mission for the home could be understood and accepted by the parents of the world, it would furnish the basis of solution for all the problems of the world.[5]

There are many ways to go about fulfilling this "transcendent mission" mentioned by President Richards. One that is readily available is that of talking. As we read in Alma: "And now, as the preaching of the word had a great tendency to lead the people to do that which was just—yea, it had had more powerful effect upon the minds of the people than the sword, or anything else, . . . therefore Alma thought it was expedient that they should try the virtue of the word of God" (Alma 31:5).

One young father and mother could see that their little boy

needed to be corrected from time to time. They did not want to impose physical pain, so they made it a practice, when discipline was necessary, to say to him, "We need to have a talk, don't we?" Then one of them would take him to another room and, with love, explain again the rules they lived by in their family. In a little while they would come walking out hand in hand, ready to try again.

This little boy was very young and had to hear some of the same talks many times. But in his teenage years, when circumstances led to surgery and much pain for this son, the parents were happy that in the times when they might have they did not inflict unnecessary sorrow in his life. Rather, because of happy times together, and also because of their talks, they have had a close relationship that has made the difficulties easier to bear.

Another way that words built a bulwark of strength for one young man was when he memorized some of them. Although most Primary children learn the Articles of Faith by the time they are twelve, this young man at four years of age could recite them perfectly. This was considered so unusual that he was often called upon to demonstrate his ability in Church meetings, which in turn gave him remarkable poise and confidence when he was very young. His parents were responsible for the memorization. Their first purpose was to see what a small child was capable of doing. They also thought that having something as positive as the Articles of Faith deeply ingrained in his mind and heart would provide a continuing guide to him.

It might well have been that foundation to his faith that kept him from fear when, as a young Scout, he was lost in the wilderness. Even after fourteen hours of wandering and searching for the trail, he did not doubt the Lord would help him. Finally, when the day was nearly spent, he saw some buildings in the far distance. His faith and his prayers were still strong. He made it to safety through the light of the Lord.

President Richards focused the following comments on the importance of bringing the Father's children safely home:

This noble concept of family life [bringing the spirit children of the Father back to his presence] places the emphasis where it truly belongs. It recognizes the value of education and parental guidance to make out of children doctors, lawyers, teachers, and artisans who can effectively serve their fellow men. All education for service and worthy accomplishment is commended, but sight is never lost, not for a moment, of the prime and ultimate objective to bring the child back to God, the Eternal Parent.[6]

One of the best evidences of parents' teaching their children to place spiritual development above the learning of the world can be seen in the vast numbers of missionaries now serving on every continent of the world. Most of these young Elders and Sisters have interrupted their educations and career training to serve the Lord in this way. The young man who began his missionary preparation by learning the Articles of Faith so early in his life was called to serve in a mission where he would need to memorize those articles and many other scriptures and teaching helps in three languages. His parents could not, perhaps, have fully envisioned how well they were preparing him.

At a Relief Society conference officers' meeting in 1959, Elder Mark E. Petersen underscored the value of teaching in the home: "As leaders, your own homes, in a sense, are the laboratories in which to prove out the best methods of family life and to develop proper examples for others. We must remember that a major part of good family life, of successful and exemplary home activity, is to teach and live the gospel in the home. The gospel must be taught there objectively. It must be lived consistently and steadily and regularly. Otherwise, the lesson is lost."[7]

One sister had a Church responsibility that required a major time commitment. She found such joy in her assignment that she felt the only thing that could bring her more happiness would be for her family, those she loved most, to have some of the same experiences she was having. Together she, her husband, their children, and their children's children planned a family conference. Dividing responsibilities, using Church programs as a guide, they planned a two-day event that brought each participant a closer feeling for family and a clearer understanding of how Church programs enhance family strength.

Some talents were discovered, some skills honed, and many hours of family fun were enjoyed by their working together to accomplish their project. Their efforts have since been extended to include family history and temple excursions, including baptisms for the dead performed by the children. This family presents an appealing picture of Latter-day Saint family togetherness, one to be hoped for.

Sometimes, however, only one parent in the home serves as an example and teacher of the gospel. If that example is sincere the lesson may not be lost. There are cases enough of a mother or a father who, with a testimony of the gospel and a commitment to the Lord, brought the children of that family (and sometimes the other parent as well) to a knowledge and love of the gospel. In a family the key is always love. To be "an example of the believers" is first of all to be loving in nature.

The Lord's crowning gift to family members who love one another is the possibility of continuing their relationships throughout eternity. Stephen L Richards spoke of this while explaining the value and uniqueness of a temple marriage:

> There is nothing anywhere comparable to the temple marriage. Temple marriage is an essential, necessary ordinance to make a man and a woman and their family eligible for exaltation in the presence of God the Father, and his Beloved Son. . . .
>
> It is difficult for many people to understand what the concept of an enduring life together means to two people who have undertaken to carry forward the great enterprise of building a home. . . .
>
> . . . Two people who constantly look forward to an eternal life together will be far more ready to forgive and to view with some tolerance the irritations that may beset their marital life. It is like a man going on a long journey. . . . He will not be too impatient about a few hours or even a few days delay . . . , but if he has an appointment [a short distance away], he gets pretty mad if road repairs hold him up for a half hour on the way. Married people who

know they have a long journey together must learn tolerance and patience.[8]

Elder Mark E. Petersen spoke of the equality of man and woman in a temple marriage, and of the blessings such a marriage brings into their home:

> So when a young couple, for example, begin their married life in the temple of God, they jointly and together enter into the same covenants under the priesthood and receive the same promises of divine beneficence.
>
> When they take this priesthood with them into their newly made homes, what does it mean?
>
> It actually means bringing God's power there—his covenant to bless that home—and his power to protect and build and sanctify it—his healing influence in times of illness—his inspiration in teaching little ones—his sanctifying influence which can make each home a temple—a place of refuge—a tabernacle of peace.
>
> When a home such as this is established, it is more than a residence where a family may eat and sleep and park the car.
>
> It is the beginning of an eternal relationship in which a family is bound together forever. . . .
>
> Spirituality comes into its own in such a family circle. There can be no true joy without God. A testimony of his great reality can come to everyone in a home such as this because God is a part of that home. His influence is there. His joy, his peace, his deep satisfactions, his prosperity, his protection, his radiated intelligence serving as a light to our minds, all are there.[9]

One family wanted their Christmas celebration to reflect their appreciation for the spirituality they felt in their home. They considered each of the traditional symbols of the Nativity, to think how they might use these to express their desired Christ-centered observance. This helped them to consider the spiritual components of Christmas.

They found great joy and enhanced meaning in their celebration. For instance, to express the light of Christmas (as when the

Wise Men followed the star that they saw appear in the east), in addition to the usual lights on their own tree they prepared *luminarios*—those lovely "bags of light" that illuminate the Mexican *posada*—and placed them along the walks in their neighborhood to spread the heavenly light.

They planned a special evening to honor the Wise Men (and Women), their grandparents. They thanked them for the gifts of so many kinds they had given the family. They recognized their grandparents' faith in the Son of God, a faith that has become a guiding light for all in the family. They acknowledged the length of their grandparents' journey through life in behalf of their faith and their family, and the many ways they continue to honor and serve the Savior.

They found many other ways to express their love for the Savior by giving gifts to those they love. These practices became their traditions of the season. They also became a way to create a greater spirit of love and reverence for the holiday time.

This family tried their best to make what they did represent their beliefs. They lived up to a standard set by President George Albert Smith: "Teach your sons and daughters to do their best and not be satisfied with something mediocre."[10]

While we may not give our all to everything we do, those things of greatest importance, of eternal significance, require our best effort. Since the goal is helping children gain eternal life, one of the ways parents or others can bless them is by teaching them how to do their best.

The Lord requires each of us to give all our heart, might, mind, and strength if we are to succeed in our eternal goals. As most of us know, our strength grows with exercise. So does our ability to bring our efforts to bear. It is difficult to give a full effort when one is unaccustomed to doing it.

Not only do our abilities grow with skillful use, but our feeling of worth also increases. "Their best" for our children finally becomes an appropriate description for their inner feelings as well as for the work they have accomplished. As President N. Eldon Tanner said:

If the senior members of the family could just realize that . . . as they meet one another, as they speak on the telephone, as they show the proper courtesy and respect for one another, they greatly influence the lives of the younger ones, I am sure they would strive to be better examples. . . .

. . . Children can be taught by the way we act, respect for one another and respect for authority. . . .

Do your children know beyond any question of doubt that the gospel means more to you than anything else in the world, that you know that it is true and that it is the plan of life and salvation, and that by living it, it will give you the greatest joy and success in this life, and that it will also prepare you to go back into the presence of our Heavenly Father?[11]

One father and mother wanted to ensure that each child in their family knew how much the gospel meant to them, and how much it influenced their lives. They wanted to be certain that the children also knew how beloved each of them was, and how often their parents remembered them in their thoughts. So they prepared a family newsletter. They included news of activities, Church events they were involved in, and expressions of their love for the family and for the Lord. Family members responded with their own news, which was included in the next issue. Family members in the mission field included their activities and testimonies. Soon each branch of the family prepared a column for every printing, complete with logo and often with pictures.

This newsletter has continued through missions and marriages. During the parents' Church assignment in a foreign country, members of the family carried on its publication. In a close family such as this one, it may be years before the real strength of this endeavor is fully realized, but already it has served as voice to the third generation. In the newsletter they have a sense of both responsibility and identity. They know that it speaks for their family. For all the members of this extended family, the newsletter has been one more bond, one more point of reference that brings vitality to their faith, strength to their family circle, and security to their individual lives.

Another family demonstrated the power of such a family bulletin at a recent family reunion. A guest at the same resort hotel observed some reunion events and was overheard telling another, in amazement, "There are a hundred of them, and they say they do this every three years!"

The woman would have been even more amazed if she had known that this family had relied almost entirely on a newsletter as their means of unity. Begun by one grandson and his wife fifteen years earlier when he was a graduate student, it has united this family of four generations and of many faiths. They became a cohesive, corresponding group that every three years travels hundreds of miles to acknowledge that which binds them together. Genealogy work is conducted, family histories shared, and hearts touched.

Elder Marion G. Romney presented a perspective on what we, with our families, could strive to attain:

> You know, sisters, if mothers and fathers would, under the direction of the Holy Spirit, strictly follow the commandments of the Lord and the counsels of his prophets to train up their children in the way they should go, the inhabitants of the earth would soon reach that glorious state enjoyed by the Nephites when "there were no contentions and disputations among them, and every man did deal justly one with another" (4 Nephi 2). . . . So blessed were they that of them the prophet-historian said, ". . . surely there could not be a happier people among all the people who had been created by the hand of God" (4 Nephi 16).
>
> Although such a blessed state seems beyond our present hope, let us not forget that the Lord has given us the assurance that the survivors of our present generation will enjoy a like society. This assurance should, and I believe it does, give us a determination to train up our children in the way they should go that they, with us, may be participants in the fulfillment of that glorious promise.[12]

7

MOTHER—
HOW NEARLY INFINITE

How nearly infinite is mother.

—*J. Reuben Clark, Jr.*

*A*t Relief Society conference, the brethren in their "instructions from time to time" often spoke to women about their importance in the eternal plan of Heavenly Father. In one such conference in 1946 President J. Reuben Clark, Jr., described the creation scene and the irreplaceable role of Mother Eve:

> So came Eve, an helpmeet to the Priesthood mission of Adam—Eve the last created being in the creation of the world, without whom the whole creation of the world and all that was in the world would have been in vain and the purposes of God have come to naught. . . .
> The Only Begotten had fashioned the world, had filled it with beautiful flowers and lofty forests, with grasses and grains, and multitudes of living creatures; Adam had had some part in this. But the key to the glorious arch of temporal, earthly creation for man was still missing. So Eve came to build, to organize, through the power of the Father, the bodies of mortal men, to be a creator of bodies under the faculties given her by the Priesthood of God, so that God's design and the Great Plan might meet fruition.[1]

President Clark described Eve's role as elevated. We note that he did not issue a competitive comparison in discussing the place of men and women. Rather, he sought to indicate the dignity of each. More important than rank order by gender is the mutual need of man and woman for each other, and it seems to be as singular for one as for the other.

With the creation of Eve we see human relationship for the first time and are told of its necessity. In an earlier address (1940) on the same subject, President Clark described the wholeness, or perfection, this relationship forms: "So began the Earth family from which we spring, the first unit organism on this earth that marks the perfect relationship between man and woman."[2]

In the 1946 address, President Clark pointed out the complexity of the human body. He spoke of the exquisite creation of each muscle, organ, and nerve, to prepare bodies through which intelligences might function in a godlike way. Some of the importance attached to the role of mother lies in the divine destiny attached to the human body. "What a miracle is motherhood," President Clark said; "how nearly infinite is mother. She fashions in her womb the most complex structure known to man, the whole visible universe being, in contrast, the simplest of creations. . . . She mounts cell on cell, each born of clay, till the normal man is brought into the world . . . , the pattern in all its infinite detail faithfully followed down to the last jot and tittle of the human frame—a body fashioned in the very image of the Son who was in the image of the Father. What an infinitely glorious concept, what a supreme destiny, and what a divine-like achievement."[3]

A mother experiences that divinity in some measure as she participates in the birth of a child. One young sister who had only recently given birth to a little daughter was attending a luncheon. Each person was asked to describe something that was to her an expression of supreme beauty in her life. When this young mother's turn came, she told of the happy expectation she felt for nine months, then of how incredibly near the Lord seemed during the actual labor and delivery. She said that the very excess of the pain seemed to bring her within reach of the source of life.

Then, she said, the peace and fulfillment of holding her newborn baby in her arms was to her the expression of supreme beauty. Such is the joy, the pain, and the privilege of being a mother, particularly a mother in Israel!

In a 1970 Relief Society conference address, President Joseph Fielding Smith taught that being a mother in Israel gives an added level of both claim and responsibility: "For us to envision what is meant by being mothers in Israel, we must have in mind our own position as the spirit children of God the Eternal Father. . . . The plan of salvation and exaltation which we know as the gospel of Jesus Christ was given to us by the Eternal Father so that we might create for ourselves eternal family units which are patterned after his family."[4]

In his address, President Smith focused on Sarah, wife of Abraham, and the blessings given her. His remarks suggest important considerations with regard to motherhood and the possible lack of it. Eve, through her choice, became a mother—by partaking of the forbidden fruit (see Genesis 3:6 and Moses 5:11). She chose to accept the resultant conditions, which included bearing children. Sarah, however, through no choice of her own, was not able to give birth during all her childbearing years. Yet in the due time of the Lord she did have a child, despite her age. Moreover, she was given extraordinary blessings regarding her posterity. Such great blessings have not, to our knowledge, been given to any of the daughters of Eve since Eve herself was called "the mother of all living" (Moses 4:26). President Smith explained:

> We are all aware that the Lord told Abraham he would be a father of many nations and that his seed would be like the stars of the heaven and as the sand which is upon the seashore in number, but what we must not overlook is that the same promises were made to Sarah.
>
> "And God said unto Abraham, As for Sarai thy wife, thou shalt not call her name Sarai, but Sarah shall her name be. And I will bless her, and give thee a son also of her: yea, I will bless her, and she shall be a mother of nations; kings of people shall be of her." [Genesis 17:15–16.][5]

While Abraham and Sarah's son was born to Sarah during her lifetime on the earth, President Smith said it was through their celestial marriage that the full blessing was accomplished: "These blessings given to Abraham and Sarah were fulfilled in and through celestial marriage, marriage for time and eternity, marriage which causes the family unit to continue and enables eternal parents to have spirit children forever in the same way that God our Heavenly Father continues to increase and abound."[6]

It is significant to note here that time was not a limiting factor to the Lord. Sarah was prepared to be a mother of nations and she received that blessing. Even as father Abraham stands as an example to all Israel of the way in which the Lord preserves and directs his people, could not mother Sarah serve as an example of how the Lord blesses women even if their need is unusual? Other women who have not given birth to children during their childbearing years—worthy, wonderful women—could see in this account of Sarah that not only does motherhood eventually come (even if it is not in this life) but there may also be abundant blessings, appropriate to them, awaiting.

Sarah's life also illustrates the interrelated role of wife and mother. For many years Sarah was a wife but not a mother. It was the way she served and fulfilled her role of wife that helped her to earn the extraordinary blessing she was given when she learned she would bear a son. There is a mutuality that exists in the most desirable relationship of a man and wife that adds a partnership to their marriage. Each one has the interest of the other at heart and tries to serve the other. Each shares in the responsibilities of the family.

This is what Elder Harold B. Lee described when he said, "A wife in a home, a woman, is expected to be . . . an intelligent and inspired participant in the family partnership."[7]

Many kinds of partnerships can be seen in marriages, beginning with the scriptural example of Eve, who "did labor with [Adam]" (Moses 5:1), and continuing on to the modern farm wife who could cook for the harvesters or ride the combine as needed, being either a side-by-side partner or a complementary one with a separate but supporting work. Examples of husband-wife relationships abound, but one of the more sensitive partnerships we have observed is of a retired couple helping one another learn to sign. *He* is losing his hearing, but it is a *partnership* we see practicing a new speech. There is no stopping place for their shared life; they will continue to support one another in whatever definition the job assumes.

Taking a view of the family that goes beyond the present, President Hugh B. Brown said: "The family concept is one of the major and most important of our whole theological doctrine. Our concept of heaven itself is little more than a projection of the home and family life into eternity. . . . In every culture, and in the widest variety of circumstances [marriage] is one of the supreme tests of human character. Laws and customs represent only the external or social aspect of marriage. No discussion of these externals can give any impression of the inwardness and depth of the problem which marriage imposes."[8]

President Brown then mentioned some of the challenges or possible problems in marriage: "Women should never allow their role as mother to overshadow their role as wife. They are both obligations divinely imposed and they should be inseparable. Neither husband nor wife can coast in on the attainments of the other; salvation is a joint undertaking, a family affair."[9]

Most of us have known of a mother who is so single-minded about responding to her childrens' every wish, or to the wishes of one child, that little time and interest remain for companionship with her husband. Such a condition can sometimes be as hurtful to the children who are the object of the attention as it is for the husband who is neglected as a result of it.

By contrast, many couples set aside a regular time for just the two of them, creating a special opportunity to nurture their companionship. One couple did this routinely by walking together. Another went to a health center together, where they shared the events of the day as they worked out on the stair climbers. One couple got home at about the same hour—one from work and the other from taking a child to the physical therapist. They couldn't always fit in a walk, so they prepared dinner together and built the strength of their relationship as they did. Of course, a regular night out together is another favorite way to promote married unity. What these couples have realized is that a marriage relationship requires care and sustenance. Love is the most needed nutrient.

While most of us have heard myriad definitions of marriage, there are still some statements that add to an understanding of its many facets. In his 1978 women's fireside address, President Spencer W. Kimball said: "Marriage is a partnership. Each is given a part of the work of life to do. The fact that some women and men disregard their work and their opportunities does not change the program. When we speak of marriage as a partnership, let us speak of marriage as a *full* partnership. We do not want our LDS women to be *silent* partners or *limited* partners in that eternal assignment! Please be a *contributing* and *full* partner."[10]

Stephen L Richards gave this perspective in relation to Latter-day Saint marriages: "A marriage is a compact between a man and wife. But a Latter-day Saint marriage carries with it something more than the worldly compact. The Latter-day Saint marriage carries the understanding that a man of the Priesthood is to stand at the head of his household."[11]

The priesthood is definitely "something more." But many outside the Mormon experience, who have not seen in practice what it can offer, may not realize that the "something more" of the priesthood is for everyone in the family and especially for the wife. As Elder Mark E. Petersen stated, its purpose is "to assure every home of God's omnipresence."[12] Through its power a worthy priesthood holder can, with authority, give blessings and counsel. However, he is also cautioned that if he attempts to use this sacred power "in any degree of unrighteousness, behold, the heavens withdraw themselves; the Spirit of the Lord is grieved; and when it is withdrawn, Amen to the priesthood or the authority of that man" (D&C 121:37).

In addition to the security of having priesthood blessings and counsel available, the wife of a worthy priesthood holder benefits from the ambience created as they seek to foster the Spirit of the Lord together. Such a woman is also in a particularly opportune position to develop her own spiritual qualities and to bring the powers of heaven close to her. President David O. McKay often urged the Saints to live spiritual lives,[13] enjoying the richness and added dimension that is missed entirely if one lives at a worldly level only. A woman who supports a man in his priesthood responsibilities and tries to be spiritually prepared along with him, and who also does acts of Christlike service, will herself become a more charitable, sacrificing, caring individual. She will develop a depth of faith and charity that is "more."

There are many examples of such inevitable improvement, but it is particularly noticeable among the wives of the General Authorities of the Church. Many of them have spent years of their lives supporting their husbands in priesthood callings yet have at the same time refined their own spirituality. We can see the strengths of their husbands mirrored in them. We find in each of them personal qualities of righteousness and individuality of character. Indeed, these attributes, both developed and innate, make them appropriate companions to their remarkable partners and, at the same time, women of distinction.

In Doctrine and Covenants 138:38–39 we read a description of the kind of partnership that will exist in the eternities for those who understand and participate as husbands and wives in this priesthood opportunity: "Among the great and mighty ones who were assembled in this vast congregation of the righteous were Father Adam, the Ancient of Days and father of all, and our glorious Mother Eve, with many of her faithful daughters who had lived through the ages and worshiped the true and living God."

To women supporting men in their priesthood responsibilities, Elder Melvin J. Ballard said: "You have been willing to do this, you have enabled men to become bishops, stake presidents, and high councilmen, and give most of their time to the Church. You are making sure that he who holds the key that shall unlock the door to your exaltation shall not lose that key; and he must magnify his calling or he will lose it. There is no power, no influence in this Church greater than that which the sisters hold, and we could not do without them."[14]

If in spite of support a husband does not assume his priesthood responsibilities, there is still fellowshipping available through quorums and bishops. President Hugh B. Brown offered a word of encouragement for sisters in such circumstances: "So I say to you, sisters, don't give up because your men are not all you would wish them to be, but maintain your faith, not only in them but in your Heavenly Father's help and your own ability to fulfill your role as a helpmate. Never cease to work and pray for divine guidance in your divine calling. Thus may you hold your families together and prepare them for the eternities to come."[15]

A woman can help her husband to live up to her hope in him. She can remember his potential and treat him with the love she feels and with respect for the priesthood she hopes he will honor. Then she may see her hopes realized. One such woman helped her children to have pride in their father and to honor, even though he did not, the priesthood that had been conferred on him. This enabled them to have a happy family and to have the children grow up honoring the priesthood that some of them would hold. The father responded to their love and respect by being a good father and husband. And with time, he also responded to their love for the gospel. He became the priesthood leader in their home that they had hoped he would be. "Love unfeigned" brings forth the power of God, from whom it emanates (see D&C 121:41).

This family knew that in lifting a person to higher performance, generous, sincere praise is more powerful than criticism. Problems can usually be identified in private. One can always be respectful of another's feelings. President Stephen L Richards said: "I always regret seeing a woman do anything to belittle her husband, even for his mistakes, before her children, and I have been hurt time and time again when I have been in homes and seen a man embarrassed, and I likewise have no sympathy with a husband who would embarrass his wife before her children. . . . So I draw that to your attention, because I believe as we preserve the integrity of the home as it was meant to be, we will do that which we should for the building up of the kingdom."[16]

Faultfinding can destroy the spirit of any home, whether it is criticism of family members, talking about someone who is not there, or complaining about leaders or programs of the Church. Criticism and finding fault have a contagion that allows them to grow in kind and amount, until they can cause harm and even heartbreak, sometimes involving many people. Cutting words inflict damage both to the victim and to the one by whom they were spoken. It is true that one individual has the power to break another's heart through unkindness, but not without hurting herself. We would do well to remember the fate of Miss Havisham of Charles Dickens's story *Great Expectations*. Although she could have been the means of doing much good, she chose to live in darkness and to promote unkindness. Finally, the very darkness and isolation she promoted led to her own destruction.

If a woman wants to very quickly improve the spirit of her home, she will refrain from faultfinding. When criticism, faultfinding, and backbiting are replaced with appreciation, compassion, and understanding, we change darkness into light.

Elder Mark E. Petersen made this appeal:

> Wouldn't you like to foster the spirit of love and prayer in your home, rather than the spirit of contention? The Savior taught us that the spirit of contention is the spirit of the devil.
>
> Let us practice our religion in the home and strive for patience, goodness, forgiveness, and long-suffering, and yet develop the courage to fight evil and put it out of our lives.
>
> Oh, sisters, let virtue garnish your thoughts unceasingly. Plan your family life so that virtue will garnish the thoughts of your children also. Be firm and courageous in standing for the right, regardless of what the world designs, or how it may beckon you into its evil pursuits.[17]

President N. Eldon Tanner said: "Now as members of [Relief Society] and as mothers in Israel, as wives and those who are neither wives nor mothers but members of the families which make up the community, you have a marvelous opportunity and a heavy responsibility of making the family and community life exemplary in every way."[18]

Elder Harold B. Lee, in the short statement, "Now, you mothers, over the Church . . . ,"[19] joined President Tanner in describing what is one of the most selfless and, in that sense, one of the most Christlike of the functions of a mother. This is the work of mothering that includes all women, and it is essential. Whatever other specific calling a woman may have—new mother, mother of teenagers, grandmother, aunt, or career woman—she can still be a "mother over the Church." This is mothering in one of its finest senses. It answers Cain's question, "Am I my brother's keeper?" (Genesis 4:9) with a resounding *yes*. And your neighbor's keeper as well. Women with this broad-reaching kind of love are concerned for the needs of others, whatever their family name. They understood the spirit of John Donne's well-known but blunt statement: "Never send to know for whom the bell tolls; It tolls for thee."[20]

One woman was neither wife nor mother, but she was a mother-over-the-Church kind of person. She taught school for many years, and saw children whose success in school was seriously hampered because of a lack of home training and family support. She manifested her concern for them by establishing first one, and then several, homes where homeless or otherwise underprivileged children could receive loving care and ordered growth in patterns of family life. The services were so effective and appreciated by the young people in these homes that she now has scores who look to her as the beloved "mother" who gave them the opportunity to succeed in life.

There are unnumbered women who have "mothered" children who are not their own, though perhaps in a less extensive way. Sometimes these are children who come from good homes but whose lives are given added richness by the interest of a caring woman. Such women, in addition to a child's own mother, may have helped with a transition in life or given reinforcement to a flagging self-esteem, or may have bolstered strength to do right just when it was needed. These special "mothers" may be women who have no children of their own, or who have a family but are willing to include others in their realm of concern.

Elder Matthew Cowley was familiar with the people of the South Pacific islands, where the spirit of caring for all children is common. He said to the sisters:

> You do not know what your own lives and your own influences mean in the lives of young people, and the lives of children. . . .
>   . . . God bless you in this great and noble work of teaching your children and the children of others the ways of righteousness, because that which you implant in youth will crop up from time to time in later life, and it may be the very influence you are wielding, of which you do not see the immediate results, that will be an anchor to the faith of these young people.
>   . . . You are the co-creators with God of his children. Therefore, it is expected of you by a right divine that you be the saviors and the regenerating force in the lives of God's children here upon the earth.[21]

One sister who is not herself a mother, but who is a favorite aunt to many, moved into a neighborhood where she had long owned property but where not all the properties nearby were being kept up as well as hers. She had recently painted her house and refurbished her garden until it was noticeably nicer than it had been. Some small children of the neighborhood came to where she was working in the flower beds. They told her they thought her house was really pretty, and asked if she had any apples she would give them to eat.

She had apples and wanted to give them to the children. But being the mothering kind of woman she was, she wanted them to learn from the experience. So she said that she was happy they liked her home and that she wondered if they noticed that one reason it was nice was that there was no trash around it. She said, "I'll help you. Let's get a bag and pick up some of the trash we can see on this street. Then the other houses will look nicer too, and then we'll get out the apples." When they had finished, she told them they could come back again and they could pick up trash and have apples then, too. They liked the new lady because she seemed to care about them.

Mother is a title that belongs to every woman by lineage from our earliest mother, Eve, and also by an eternal destiny. Every woman can learn how the designation fits her life and how to find glory in it. Then she might see the fruition of her labors as similar to that of many women worldwide who are on God's side, who do seemingly small things that are of great worth in carrying forward his work. All of us can be on his side if we prepare our hearts to receive his revealed word and then keep his commandments. Then love will quickly spread from heart to heart, touching the varied facets of each Latter-day Saint home. Surely this is the desire of every sister in Zion. As President Hugh B. Brown said: "When the opportunity to serve is recognized as a blessing, where thoughtfulness, courtesy, tolerance, kindness, consideration are habitual, where duties become privileges, where virtues are recognized and gratefully mentioned, where faults are minimized or overlooked, where the home is enveloped by love and hallowed by prayer, there is heaven on earth, and there eternal homes are in the making. To foster such homes is the most effective part of your service to the Church."[22]

8

COMPETENT MOTHERS:
THE WORLD'S GREATEST NEED

A competent mother in every home is the greatest need of the world today.

—David O. McKay

*M*uch has been written, said, and sung about the role of mother and her irreplaceable function in bringing a child into the world. We praise the value of the care and training she can give. But it is most critical that a woman who is herself a mother believe this. President David O. McKay attests, "In her high duty and service to humanity . . . she is co-partner with the Creator Himself."[1] Hers is a calling whose exceptional joy in fulfillment can be matched only by the compassion and tireless devotion with which it is undertaken.

President Anthony W. Ivins, in setting a context for his remarks about mothers, reflected upon a scene he observed on the lawn outside his window:

> Yesterday, as I was at work in my room in the Church Office Building, I heard a baby voice saying, "Ma! Ma! Ma!" I went to the north window, and there on the lawn, with a woman's coat under it, I saw a baby sitting. Naturally the child attracted my attention, and I stood looking at it. In a few moments a woman, frail

looking, came round the corner of the building, went to the baby, and gathered it up in her arms. A little girl, whose head came to the mother's shoulder, was walking by her side, and three little boys, each with a cheap toy in his hands, trotted along behind. Gathering up the child, the mother said, "Come along, boys," and started out toward the street.

The whole story was told to me as I stood there looking. The woman was comfortably, but rather poorly clothed. The clothing of the children was ordinary, but looked comfortable. They all appeared to be happy. As I stood there I offered a prayer of thanksgiving to God our Father for women, for mothers, for women who were ready to take up the responsibility of wifehood, of motherhood, of life, even under adverse circumstances, giving, as I knew this little woman had, her life for those children.

. . . I do not know who she was or is, but I felt like going out and blessing her.[2]

President Ivins then said that if he were given the responsibility to establish an empire or a kingdom, he would want just such women as that woman, and similarly humble men, to go with him to accomplish the undertaking—"women of faith, of devotion, women who are willing to make sacrifice, women from whom their faith could not be purchased with the wealth of the world."[3]

Another woman that we observed reminded us that the young mother President Ivins saw was typical of many who are willing to give up personal advantage for their children. Her sacrifice, if not of all the wealth of the world, was of a modest personal income. She and her husband had just had their first baby. Conveniently, the baby had been born in the summer when the mother, a first-grade teacher, could devote her full time to his care. As fall approached, she made arrangements to have someone care for the baby so she could return to teaching. But as the time for school neared, she thought of all the subtle ways she was sensitive to her little boy's needs—his moods, his cries, and his playful times. She realized that another might not see such things as well. She thought of how she would miss him. She envisioned the things he soon would be able to do if she could help him. She became increasingly sure that as much as she loved her job and would miss those little children who came to her so eager to learn, she could not choose to leave her baby and the closeness of spirit they shared. She called school officials to notify them, and was relieved to learn that someone well qualified to take her place in the classroom was available and anxious for the job. She then was free to do what she knew no one else could do as well—to be the mother to her baby.

In a 1955 Relief Society conference address, President J. Reuben Clark, Jr., spoke on what the scriptures tell us about children. He read passages from 3 Nephi in which the Savior asked the Nephites to bring their children to him. After giving each child a blessing, he told the multitude to look, and "they saw the heavens open, and they saw angels descending out of heaven as it were in the midst of fire" to minister to the children (3 Nephi 17:24).

One mother who understood the value of being aware of her child's spiritual nature tried to see perceptible ways in which her baby's inner feelings were reflected. She observed that, given quiet time to become acquainted with the world into which he had come, her baby contented himself. Rather than rushing to pick him up at the first sound that indicated he had awakened in the morning, this mother simply checked to see that he was all right. Then she allowed the baby to greet the morning in his own way: cooing, gurgling, and responding to the sights around him. The mother, in her love for her child, helped him find a calm morning peace to set the tone for his day.

Some other babies might not respond well to a quiet time in the morning. But the important thing we see with this mother is her personal ministering to her infant's individual need. We can learn from the visit of the Savior to the Nephites that there is concern in the heavens for every child. Those whose privilege it is to care for children here on earth can bring to that care a heavenly spirit with which babies are at home.

Explaining one of the passages he shared from 3 Nephi, President Clark said:

> This shows how precious in the sight of the Lord are the children which we have. And may I remind you, these children did not come to you and ask you to give them bodies, they did not ask you sisters to become mothers and the men to become fathers of their earthly bodies. The Lord commanded, of course, that we should multiply and replenish the earth. But you, of your own volition, created the bodies for the spirits to take, and these little ones were gracious enough to come to the body you created. They are your guests. You, as hosts, owe to them all of the consideration, all of the love, all of the kindness, all of the patience and courtesy and all the other virtues that it is possible for you to give. They are here because you invited them to come. Thank God for their presence.[4]

Most parents are thankful for their children, but one father and mother showed they were so in a special way. They had three healthy children. Caring for them was a continuing process of rewarded hope, as it is with most children who are healthy and responsive. One development followed after another in an ongoing cycle of growth and reward. Then, when their fourth child was about nine months old, its development stopped. The medical world could neither explain nor cure the condition, yet the child no longer responded, no longer developed. Two other children were born to the couple, and these children were similarly afflicted.

Learning the truth of this condition brought heartbreak, then adjustment as the parents began finding special ways to meet the needs of their children. Despite all of the sadness at seeing the three youngest children so impaired in their progress and so hampered in their ability to enjoy life, the family, of course, loved them anyway. They did all in their power to make their earthly lives meaningful and happy. Manifestations of the Spirit told them the children were beloved of our Father in Heaven and known to him. While their family life has been difficult, the parents feel blessed and believe that they have become closer to the Savior than they might have been had all their children been healthy. They do thank God for *all* their children.

President Hugh B. Brown talked about being able to handle trials as they come. He pointed out that they will come, and none need think they can be spared from the lessons that trials have to teach.

Those lessons can sometimes be learned gently in small ways when children are young. One little girl was sensitive to the principle of perfection and was working to implement it. On a particular evening she declared to all in the family that tomorrow would be her perfect day. She chose the dress she would wear and laid it out, picked out matching socks, polished her shoes, and put books, pencil, comb, hair ribbon, everything in a special place, ready. Later, just as she was going to sleep, she called from her room, "Remember, tomorrow is my perfect day!"

Tomorrow dawned and things went well for a while. Then, because all didn't happen in the way she had planned, there were tears. It wasn't perfect. With love, praise, and prayer, she finally went to school smiling, knowing that even trying to be perfect was pleasing to Heavenly Father. She realized also that whatever our frustrations and defeats, we can turn to him for strength to go on. She was beginning to learn that perfection comes not as much through insisting upon our plans as through following well the Lord's plans for us. She would come to know more about his will and ours.

President Brown urged:

> Let each Relief Society worker ask herself whether she is pro-
> viding, first, the spiritual foundations for her children, foundations
> upon which they may build the superstructure which will stand at
> the last day when the winds of doubt and confusion beat upon
> their house, when only those founded upon the rock of eternal
> truth shall stand. . . . One of the most inspiring thoughts in this
> connection is that the storms beat upon the house that is on the
> rock as well as the one on the sand, and the fact that your house is
> built upon the rock will not excuse you from the lessons that the
> storms have to teach.[5]

The wail of a siren always cries, "Emergency!" It is unnerving whenever it is heard, but when it signals the approach of an ambulance to aid a loved one it often leaves a waiting family member in a state that is past feeling. Such was the state of a husband when his wife of more than fifty years collapsed and slipped into unconsciousness. The siren wailed. The ambulance came. Expert technicians knew immediately what to do for her, and that was what he truly wanted. But at the hospital, as they carried her away, his vitality seemed to leave with her. He waited motionless, spent. Only as their children began to gather at the hospital did his strength revive. Each of the five came as quickly as possible and was there at his side. Together they felt the peace of the Lord in the strength of a family united in faith and in their prayers for their mother. They knew that now, as always, when problems came they could look to the Lord and trust in his power and wisdom. These things their mother, for whom they now prayed, had taught them at her knee.

Elder Marion G. Romney said:

When I think of Relief Society sisters, I think of Latter-day Saint mothers in Latter-day Saint homes surrounded by their children. The contemplation of this sacred sanctuary brings to mind the Lord's instructions for us to bring up our "children to light and truth" (D&C 94:40). . . . For our purposes here, we have but time to say that truth embraces knowledge. As you know, the Prophet defined it—"knowledge of things as they are, and as they were, and as they are to come . . ." (D&C 93:24). These are the great truths which the gospel teaches. Light connotes forsaking of evil. Therefore, to bring up children in "light and truth," we must teach them the word of God and inspire them to forsake evil.

I need not elaborate on the theme that children become about what their mothers make them. . . . This is illustrated in the tribute paid to their mothers by the 2,000 young men referred to in The Book of Mormon as the Sons of Helaman. At a time when they were faced with overwhelming odds, Helaman asked them if they would go against the enemy to battle. Although they were very young, they answered,

... behold our God is with us, and he will not suffer that we should fall; then let us go forth; we would not slay our brethren if they would let us alone; therefore let us go, lest they should overpower the army of Antipus.

Now they never had fought, yet they did not fear death; and they did think more upon the liberty of their fathers than they did upon their lives; yea, they had been taught by their mothers, that if they did not doubt, God would deliver them.

And they rehearsed . . . the words of their mothers, saying: We do not doubt our mothers knew it (Alma 56:46–48).

Without a knowledge of the word of God, these noble mothers never could have built into their sons such an abiding conviction that "if they did not doubt, God would deliver them"; and neither could they have inspired in their sons an unshakeable faith that their "mothers knew" what they were talking about.

My beloved sisters, for the salvation of yourselves, your children, and your children's children, I urge you to get a knowledge of the principles of the gospel and impart the knowledge to your children in your home. It is a mistake to depend solely upon the Church organizations to give them this knowledge. Yours is the primary and the final responsibility to bring up your children in "light and truth."[6]

For one family their home was the Church. They were the only permanent Latter-day Saint family living in a small costal community. For many years, meetings were held and missionaries gathered in their home. The mother of the family was a dynamic teacher. She loved the gospel, especially the story of the Prophet Joseph Smith and the restored Church. Each time the family had a visitor or the missionaries brought an investigator, she taught a lesson including this story. One of her sons remembers hearing the recounting of that history more times than he can number. It may never be known how many of those who heard it for the first time were persuaded by the message, but her children were thoroughly convinced. They have taught it, written about it, and lived by the truths it embodied through all of their lives.

Her children are uncertain if their mother was telling the

story again and again just for the visitors and investigators, or whether she was also telling it for *them* to hear. She did not live to see them fully grown and married. Maybe she somehow knew that she needed to make sure the story of the restored gospel was forever engraved upon their hearts.

President Heber J. Grant had a mother who made a great difference to him. He always acknowledged her help: "As you have heard me say many times, for that which I have accomplished in the battle of life I give credit to my mother first and foremost. In my observations I have found that many men who have been successful in the battle of life are indebted principally to the example, the energy, and untiring labors of faithful mothers."[7]

Elder Harold B. Lee said to the sisters: "I say to you mothers, if you ever have sons and daughters who amount to what they should in the world, it will be in no small degree due to the fact that your children have a mother who spends many nights on her knees in prayer, praying God that her son, her daughter, will not fail." He then went on to tell of his mother's help as she warned him of an impending temptation in his life when he was a teenager.[8]

A mother may feel that her personal prayers, because they are private, are unknown to her family. This may not be the case. One young man came to his mother disturbed by a problem that was out of his power to control. After talking about possible consequences and what he could do, she then said, "Son, do you know what I would do if I had that problem?"

"Of course I do," he said. "You'd pray about it."

Surprised at his immediate answer, the mother asked how he could know that. Her son replied, "Because I *know* you, Mother."

He also knew what to do about his problem even before he asked, but perhaps he needed the confirmation of her faith in his prayers. A mother's prayers may be instructions to her children as well as petitions to the Lord.

President David O. McKay spoke of another way to influence children for good in the home:

Sisters, apply your influence to have more religion in your homes. Every Latter-day Saint home should have evidences therein of the family membership. A successful man once wrote:

> My father came into my house soon after I was married and looked around. I showed him into every room, and then in his rough way he said to me, "Yes, it is very nice, but nobody will know walking through here whether you belong to God or to the devil." I went through and looked at the rooms again, and I thought he is quite right.

There is a lesson. Children growing up should come in contact with things religious. I ask you now, have you in your home the Church works, ready at hand so that the children going to Sunday School, Primary, Mutual Improvement, and so on, can turn to them when they need them? Have you a religious verse in the bedroom of the boys, or a saying of the Savior? I wonder if you have a good painting of the Savior hanging up over the bed of your boy. Little things like these give to home a religious atmosphere.[9]

A lovely and hopeful bride-to-be was making plans for establishing what she wanted to become a true Latter-day Saint home. She said to a younger sister, "Would you please send a subscription for the Church magazines to start coming to my new house immediately? I want them to always be there, so that we never have to decide whether we will subscribe or not. Then they will be a part of what our home is from the beginning."

In the scriptures we can read the line ". . . and terrible as an army with banners" (D&C 5:14). What makes an army with banners a terrifying foe? They have declared their colors, they know with whom they stand, and they have visible evidence of their cause. This young bride knew the strength of a declaration of faith, of taking a stand. She was aware of the power it brings to a cause. When the Church magazines arrive in a home, the person who unwraps them has in his or her hand, and places on a table for all to see, a banner of the family's colors. It speaks of the faith that is in them. They are strong as it is strong.

President J. Reuben Clark, Jr., gave sobering counsel about providing every learning advantage to the children who are ours to protect:

Never forget that Satan stands at the very elbow of each of your sons and daughters, he awaits outside the threshold of every home, every minute of the day, waiting for, seeking for the slightest weakness in the armor of righteousness with which you have clad your loved ones, with which you have surrounded your home; so that against that weakness he may bring to bear every vile, every stratagem, every base feeling and appeal—and he has every evil at his command. . . .

Mothers in Israel, in that home which it is in your power and which it is your duty to build, that home of bodily well-being, that home of love, and prayer and precept and example, of harmony, of seemliness and respect, and education and culture, bring into that home such an understanding and reverence for chastity as shall preserve your children.[10]

From the point of view of one who had seen and knew, Elder Hugh B. Brown, in a 1943 *Relief Society Magazine* article, told how letters from home are often the means of safeguarding sons and daughters who are away. Speaking of young men in active military service, he said:

They must know—and you must tell them—that they are trusted, that you have no doubt of the quality of their manhood and the integrity of their character. They will respond to the trust you place in them, will strive to be worthy of your confidence. They will spread their wings to the lifting power of your faith in them.

They hunger and thirst for word from home and anxiously watch for the arrival of the mail. If you could be present at a mail delivery in a desert camp and see their eager and expectant faces as they wait for their names to be called; if you could note, as we have done, the dejection and utter loneliness of the few to whom no mail has come, and see them crawl into their pup tents, homesick to the marrower marrow of their bones; if you could know, as Satan knows, that at such moments their resistance is at low ebb, and that it is then he can get in some of his most effective work, you would make sure that every week would see at least one letter on its way to them. . . .

. . . Nothing which the Church may do can take the place of letters of love and encouragement from home.

But we must not write letters which have a depressing effect upon our sons. We should not emphasize the worries and despondencies which may annoy us at the time of writing. Nor should we criticize the conduct of the war or our leadership in our letters, as confidence and loyalty are basic to effective military service. Our letters should be buoyant, cheerful, full of hope. They should carry the contagion of a triumphant spirit.[11]

Elder Brown served as coordinator for LDS servicemen during World War II and was deeply concerned for those in military service. His appeal, however, is just as vital for mothers of sons and daughters serving on missions. With only a minimal change of wording the message applies. It could almost be said that missionaries serve well in direct proportion to the quality of support they receive from home. Their circumstance is a kind of battlefront, the enemy is real, and the defeats frequent. Letters from home help dress the wounds and give a missionary courage to go out and try again.

Note the experience of two well-fortified Elders who were able to handle crushing defeat one rainy day, oceans away from home on the small island of Tasmania.

This was to be the day of a baptism, their first in weeks. They went early to the chapel to start filling the font, then got on their bicycles to go to the home. It had been a difficult conversion, with much negative influence from others, but finally the mother and her daughter had concluded to follow their hearts and be baptized. The elated missionaries hurried up the walk to their investigators' home, but could hardly believe what they saw. A note on the door read, "We are sorry we cannot go through with our plans. Please do not come back." During the hours since the Elders had last seen them, someone had talked to the mother and young girl and weakened their resolve. The devastated Elders rode their bikes to an alleyway nearby. They stopped for a few minutes, cried, bore their testimonies to each other, then rode off to empty the font and try to find someone else who might listen. Thanks in part to the love and support they received in letters from home, both young men knew the Church was true. They both knew they had the strength to go on, to keep working and to make their families proud of their courage.

"I believe a competent mother in every home is the greatest need of the world today," said President David O. McKay in a 1936 Relief Society conference address. A bit further on in this same talk, he declared: "It seems to me that the adaptation of knowledge and skill to the building of a beautiful home is the highest of attainments. In the true sense of the word, therefore, we are justified in speaking of home-building as an art. . . . By the art of home-building, I mean the inculcating in the lives of children a nobility of soul that leads them instinctively to love the beautiful, the genuine, the virtuous, and as instinctively to turn from the ugly, the spurious, and the vile."[12]

One young man displayed this kind of strength. It led him to do something unusually kind and gave evidence of the quality of his home.

Several families in the neighborhood had gathered in an open play area for games. One family, having moved into their home only a short while before, was new to the others. One of their children had recently undergone surgery that left him lame in one leg and without the use of one arm and hand.

As the games were getting under way, there were shouts of "Line up for a three-legged race!" This remarkable young man, an acknowledged leader among the young people, was a little older and stronger than the disabled boy. He hurried over before anyone had chosen partners for the race, and in a voice that all could hear called, "Come on, you and I can win this one!"

He could not have known how his immediately choosing this lame boy to be his partner turned the world around for the boy. It did the same for his parents, who were there and so anxious for their son. And it didn't happen just once. The young man continued to brighten the life of the sometimes lonely boy, simply by being his friend.

Much could be said about what a mother can or should do in her home. But nothing speaks so clearly of the quality of living and loving that takes place inside a house as the unprompted behavior of a son. Nothing tells so well that the gospel has become the way and the light.

In words we would all do well to remember, President Hugh B. Brown spoke to women about priority and piety, but even more about divine purpose: "In what work then can you best make contributions to the program of the Church? First, and most importantly, you make a contribution as mothers and teachers—two of the highest and most sacred callings in all life. These callings require sanctification. You remember the Master said, 'And for their sakes I sanctify myself, that they also might be sanctified through the truth' (John 17:19)."[13]

9

CHARITY—
A CROWN OF LOVE

Let kindness, charity and love crown your works.

—*Joseph Smith*

$\mathcal{A}$nn White joined the Church in England, made her way to America, and became part of the James Jepsen wagon company, soon heading west. At twenty-three she was a frail woman, but she walked the full distance from Winter Quarters to the valley of the Great Salt Lake. For Ann the arrival in the valley marked an abrupt change in plans. The young man to whom she was engaged was not content to stay in the settlements. He wanted to go on to California with those who were eager for gold. Ann chose not to go. She told her fiancé that she had sacrificed all her material belongings for the gospel, and that it was of more worth to her than all that gold could bring. He went on. She stayed with the Saints.

Elder Mark E. Petersen said: "I have learned that there is a feminine side to spirituality which we men seldom, if ever, truly appreciate. That feminine type of spirituality is truly divine. It is what makes good mothers great. It is what makes them partners with God in a very real and literal sense. It is what makes them the queens of their homes, the spiritual centers of their families."[1]

While Ann and her fiancé are only one example among many hundreds, we can see in their lives a little of what Elder Petersen spoke about. She was able to see, where her fiancé could not, the richer value that lay in committing their lives to building the Lord's kingdom rather than seeking their own fortunes.

A man named Samuel Bradshaw learned of the broken engagement. He was attracted to Ann, the English girl, and proposed marriage to her. She thought it over for a time, agreed, and they were wed.

Elder Petersen continued his observations:

> To nurture this feminine factor in spirituality, a woman needs a woman's spiritual contact just as a man for his masculine type of faith, needs the power of the Priesthood quorum. Women need to unite with other women in the development of their own spiritual natures. They need to unite with other women of like faith and spirituality to obtain the added strength to take their place as the center of faith and devotion among their children. Knowing this, the Lord provided a special women's organization for his faithful daughters. It was established by the Prophet Joseph Smith.[2]

Along with being an effective working force in worthy causes, the sisterhood of Relief Society is a vital strength to the women themselves. It provides for bonding with other sisters in a setting compatible with spiritual development. By sharing their faith and combining their efforts Relief Society women become stronger as individuals. Some say that a woman is at risk of loneliness or ineffective social relations if she does not do some social bonding. Relief Society offers this to her, along with essential spiritual reinforcement.

Elder Gordon B. Hinckley recognized the value of the sisters serving together. United in a cause, they forget self and become better persons. He stated:

> While women, by nature, are more prone to kindness, to understanding and sympathy, one need not look far to recognize that those virtues become easily buried, and may not find expression

without the kind of motivation that comes through the Relief Society. This is the organization in the Church whose objective is compassionate service, and the never-failing result is that as women forget themselves in service, they inevitably develop those great virtues which crown their lives with saintliness. . . .

It will be so with all who, under the program of this organization, will labor in compassionate service to others. Selfishness will be subdued, and with it will come a blossoming of virtue that will bless the homes and the families and communities of those who serve.[3]

To Elder Hinckley's promise, which surely speaks to the soul of every earnest Relief Society sister, we add this statement of Elder George Albert Smith to the sisters of Relief Society: "You are to be congratulated that you possess the knowledge that every good thing that the people of the world enjoy, you may enjoy, and in addition that you may draw near to your Heavenly Father in prayer, and begin the consecration of your lives right here on earth and be prepared for eternal happiness in the Celestial Kingdom."[4]

Speaking of the early days of Relief Society, Elder Marion G. Romney said: "To be prepared to carry forward their great work, the women were to first purify themselves. [The Prophet Joseph Smith] warned them to beware of self-righteousness. 'Be limited,' he said, 'in the estimate of your own virtues and not think yourselves more righteous than others. You must enlarge your souls towards each other.'"[5]

One sister had an unusual struggle in this regard. She found life frustrating because she was so intent upon perfection—her own perfection—that any failure at all, even the slightest weakness, gave her feelings of despair that she had difficulty setting aside. As she turned inward, she lost the very enjoyment she might have experienced by helping others and forgetting her own problems. She became dejected, intensifying her misery.

Prayer proved to be her means of regaining spiritual perspective. She remembered that "the Lord will judge all men according to their works, according to the desire of their hearts" (D&C 137:9). This let her realize that in evaluating our individual progress we should consider not only our best efforts but also the desire of our hearts. Meanwhile, we can become one with the Lord through service in his cause.

Elder Bruce R. McConkie reminded the sisters, "To become like him, we have to have the same character, perfections, and attributes that he possesses."[6]

Inasmuch as we all need to be in search of those attributes, President George Albert Smith mentioned in a kindly way a specific fault we must carefully guard against: "I wonder if we realize that if we tell a story about our neighbor, . . . if we say something to injure him, not telling the truth, that we violate one of the loving counsels of the Father of us all. He said we should not do that, and if we do, we do not gain anything, we always lose."[7]

One sister was on guard against evil-speaking. She prepared a good defense against it. On a social occasion she and her husband joined in a group that was talking. Soon the conversation drifted into criticism of some people who were not present. After only one or two remarks it was evident that hurtful things were being said. While the comments were not actually untrue, they were not intended to help but only to be heard—some talk is like that. The sister quickly said to her husband, but within the hearing of all, "Dear, I think we have brought a negative spirit with us. We had better leave." She was sincere; others were chagrined. The subject was quickly changed.

"Don't gossip about matters relating to your sisters," counseled Elder Harold B. Lee. "Never remember nor publicize what you do for another, but never forget a favor a sister renders to you. Yes, be loyal to each other, as sisters in the gospel of the kingdom."[8]

Being loyal is not only for Boy Scouts. A true friend is a treasure to be cherished, and all can be true friends. Loyalty is probably a learned characteristic, but for the willing and determined it is not hard to learn. And it is impossible to think of a Christlike person who doesn't possess that quality.

One mother found an opportunity to teach her daughters about loyalty to family. The girls, along with a sleep-over friend, were playing with the neighborhood children in the yard next door. The younger of the two sisters suffered some mistreatment by some of the youngsters, causing her to run home crying. After hearing her complaints, her mother called the older sister home. She asked why she hadn't come home too. The older girl thought that because she hadn't been involved, she didn't need to be concerned. But her mother explained that if her sister was hurt by what the others did, it affected her too.

"This is being loyal to your sister," she said. "The next time something like this happens, try to remember that if you cannot work out the problem there, you will be her friend and come home with her."

The sleep-over guest was only an observer to all of this, but she never forgot the lesson on loyalty and what it means to be a sister.

From the specifics of personal preparation to carry forward the work of the Lord, we next learn more about the place of Relief Society in the gospel plan. With his knowledge of the law—particularly here the law of heaven—Elder Marion G. Romney carefully related the relationship of Relief Society to that law: "In the meeting of March 17, 1842, in which the Prophet Joseph Smith organized the Relief Society, it is reported that President John Taylor said he 'rejoiced to see this institution organized according to the law of heaven.'"[9]

Then Elder Romney continued by telling exactly why he thought President Taylor rejoiced:

> I think his words were carefully chosen and deliberately spoken. . . . He had a profound understanding of the significance of what had been done. I think he rather fully realized the potentialities of this great organization, and that he did, in fact, rejoice in its organization according to the law of heaven. . . .
>
> It is altogether understandable that John Taylor, with his understanding, faith, and expectations, would be alert and sensitive to what was going on as he saw and heard the Prophet organize the Relief Society, and he understood Joseph's statements that "the Lord has something better for them than a written constitution." . . .

The Prophet also declared to the sisters that they would

> . . . receive instructions from the order of the priesthood which God has established, through the medium of those appointed to lead, guide and direct the affairs of the Church in this last dispensation. . . . (*A Centenary of Relief Society,* p. 16.)

> . . . And the Prophet further stated that if they needed his instruction, to ask him and he would give it "from time to time." These statements opened to the mind of John Taylor new visions of the role that women were to play in the building of Zion.
> He fully realized that a society "under the Priesthood after a pattern of the Priesthood"—which Priesthood he knew to be the power and the pattern of government by which and under which God himself orders and controls the universe—was indeed "organized according to the law of heaven." He knew that the "something" which the Lord had for the sisters—which would be "better for them than a written constitution"—was the guidance of the living oracles of God—those Priesthood bearers with whom God himself communicates and through whom he directs his work in the earth. Such a constitution, he knew, would give the Relief Society guidance superior to that enjoyed by any other female organization in the earth.[10]

For the evidence of this guidance we can look at the constant growth of the organization in both size and effectiveness. It now functions on every continent of the earth. At this writing, the membership is nearly three and a half million. The influence of the Lord guides Relief Society wherever it is found, and a glimpse into any one of the units would reward the viewer with manifestations of the Lord's Spirit.

In one university stake, this worldwide program could be seen serving a local need. The student wards assumed a compassionate service project of visiting elderly women in rest homes. These young sisters, most of whom had not been to Relief Society before, went regularly to visit the women; they read to them, wrote letters for them, and sometimes just visited. They learned that many of the older sisters had been quilters in earlier times, and that they missed this favorite craft and had little to take its place. The older sisters had not thought they could do quilting in their rest home.

The students wanted to help. They decided to try putting up a quilt. They found to their delight and to that of the older women, that with the young sisters to set up the frames and thread the needles, the women could quilt. The students were excited and pleased. These lovely older women, so like their own grandmothers or great-grandmothers, eagerly took up their needles and enjoyed again the sociability and conversation that quilting together revived. The rest home residents seemed to come alive with their stitching. They loved teaching the young sisters how to quilt. The time the women spent together was stimulating for the older ones, who found a new vitality, and for the younger ones who had the joy of helping and of finding that they were learning as well. The activity seemed to fulfill the scripture, "all things work together for good to them that love God" (Romans 8:28).

When Relief Society was born there were many acts of kindness, attributes of godliness, and attitudes of charity also waiting to be born. But first women were needed—women of commitment with the desire to do the Lord's will. "The Lord requireth the heart and a willing mind" (D&C 64:34).

With the women came their offerings, and as President Joseph Fielding Smith said:

> The good that has been accomplished in the care of the poor, care of the sick and the afflicted, and those who are in physical, mental, or spiritual need, will never correctly be known. This, however, need not be our concern. The main interest lies in the fact that all of this has been accomplished through the spirit of love in accordance with the true spirit of the gospel of Jesus Christ. It is clear to see that without this wonderful organization, The Church of Jesus Christ of Latter-day Saints never could have been completely organized.[11]

President J. Reuben Clark, Jr., added emphasis to other statements about the importance of Relief Society: "This unique qualification of priesthood blessing and promise that is yours, that sets you apart from all other organizations, and that gives you a power and authority that no other woman's organization in the world possesses, brings with it certain duties and responsibilities which largely determine and fix your work."[12]

On another occasion President Clark described the work of the Society in the following terms: "In all that relates to the infinities of kindly attention and sympathy, in all that relates even remotely to the love and ritual of motherhood, the Women's Relief Society carries the burden. . . . They encourage the heavily burdened and despondent, they hold up the hands of the fainthearted, they sweep despair out of the hearts of the distressed, they plant hope and faith and righteousness in every household."[13]

One household will always remember how necessary that faith and hope are. For them, the faith of the family and priesthood blessings in which they had trust, were critical in the healing of a beloved three-year-old daughter. One day, just after her mother had helped her into a starched white pinafore, she walked too close to an open flame. The end of her sash caught fire, quickly igniting all her clothing. Though she had help immediately, she was severely burned.

The little girl's condition was grave. The day of her accident the mother's grandfather, an apostle of the Lord, gave the child a blessing. The family had great trust in that blessing. When he came to the hospital again a few days later saying that he had come to give her another blessing, the little girl's mother said, "But grandfather, you gave her a blessing last week."

To this the grandfather replied, "I know, but I have a blessing to give her today. And I can't tell you how important it is that I give her this blessing." He continued coming and giving blessings until she was clearly better.

Although it was nine months before they had their little girl home again, the sister said that they were more thankful than they could say for the blessings, for the caring, and for her life. She also said she was thankful for spiritual preparation, which had fortified her for such a difficult time.

Elder Levi Edgar Young said: "The members of the Relief Society of the Church go among the people who suffer in their feelings; who need the blessings of human helpfulness; who crave for some loving word in time of death; who hunger for some blessing in days of sorrow. They are messengers of happiness to the oppressed and the needy. They love mercy. They show mercy. It is their action of love and charity that brings the most subtle and tingling sense of happiness that can be felt by any human being. It is a conduct of life built up by faith and a feeling of joy which comes from service to mankind."[14]

A kindness we may not think of as service was expressed by one sister who said she appreciated someone's taking time to share a spiritual experience with her. A convert to the Church, she was trying to learn all she could. Sometimes questions came to her mind. When she asked those about her for answers, she was told, "Oh, you can only know that by the Spirit." But she didn't know *how* to know by the Spirit. Finally one of the sisters told her about a spiritual experience she had recently had. She talked with this new member about how the Spirit often gives us answers to what we have prayed about. And she told her that although experiences of the Spirit are sacred, they can be shared at appropriate times.

Especially in our current world, we all need to be fortified spiritually. There is much each of us can do, as President Joseph Fielding Smith stated, "I say there is no limit to the good that our sisters can do."[15]

However, it is a large mission and may seem more than we are able to fulfill, but a focus on individuals that gives rise to specific action and meets immediate needs is realistic. Elder Marion G. Romney gave this counsel:

No soul desires and deserves appreciation more than your own family, your intimate acquaintances, and your neighbors, old or young, rich or poor. It is the duty of Relief Society members and all Church members to look to and purify themselves, to love and to care for, encourage and appreciate the members of their own household, and to extend that love to their neighbors.

This is an area in which we get into a sphere of action where no bishop can tell us just what to do. No person other than ourselves can solve our individual problems or direct our specific actions because conditions change and vary. However, principles governing character building and spiritual growth do not change. They persist eternally. We must act on those principles if we would have joy in performing our duty. This is the area where we act, not as an organization, but as members of the Relief Society. We act according to the principle pronounced by the Lord in the 58th Section of the Doctrine and Covenants where he said:

> . . . it is not meet that I should command in all things; for he that is compelled in all things, the same is a slothful and not a wise servant; wherefore he receiveth no reward. Verily I say, men should be anxiously engaged in a good cause, and do many things of their own free will, and bring to pass much righteousness; For the power is in them, wherein they are agents unto themselves. And inasmuch as men do good they shall in nowise lose their reward (D&C 58:26–28).[16]

In our day people live increasingly longer. Some older sisters outlive their years of being needed by so many for so much, then languish in inactivity with a feeling of purposelessness. Yet they are a part of the Lord's family, as dear to him as any of his children. Like all of us, they need each day to find a brightness of hope. Some sisters recognize this need and respond with compassion.

One sister determined to do what she could to increase the joy in life for an elderly woman living nearby in a relative's home. Although she was a busy, active woman with children at home, she made time and took opportunity to bring to the elderly sister craft projects they could do together. She took the older sister to concerts with her family, for afternoon rides to feed the ducks, to tour a fire station where there was a commemorative open house, and to homemaking meetings where she often helped her with projects. Through her efforts she created for this elderly sister a bright and sparkling life within a life that was otherwise mostly lackluster. How much real difference can one person make in another person's life? This sister's loving concern is a never-to-be-forgotten example.

Another sister, this time the daughter of an older sister, sacrificed to make the last days of her mother's life as nearly what the mother wanted as she could. The mother desired, for example, to stay in the home where she had lived with her family all her married years. Although it was in another town and a considerable distance to travel, the daughter arranged for her mother to stay there and to have twenty-four-hour care. But more than that, she spent one day and night every week with her mother to be certain that she was well and happy and that she knew of the daughter's love and concern for her. When the mother's health permitted, the daughter arranged outings for her, took her to visit her friends, or arranged for the friends to visit her. Although she had a full calendar of activities, a husband, grandchildren, and children who also claimed her attention, she devotedly attended to her mother's needs.

These sisters are typical of many who look around them to see who they can help and then minister in the compassionate way the gospel teaches.

Elder Gordon B. Hinckley spoke of such people and their attitude that lifts others, particularly with regard to their influence in their homes:

> But there is a more subtle and a more important factor in strengthening the homes of our people. It is an intangible quality, the cultivation of an attitude that [graces] . . . a woman . . . with touches of the higher virtues—sacrifice, understanding, sympathy, encouragement, and integrity. These, in turn, become reflected in the lives of her children.
>
> I am convinced that it is the diminishing presence of these virtues in the homes of the world that accounts, in large measure, for the deterioration of law and order among the youth of many nations.
>
> Thank the Lord for this great organization [the Relief Society] which is training the women of the Church—wherever they take advantage of its program—not only to beautify their homes, but, more importantly, to strengthen the spirit and improve the influence of those homes.

On April 28, 1842, Joseph Smith, speaking to that first Relief Society group, admonished: "When you go home, never give a cross . . . word . . . but let kindness, charity, and love crown your works henceforth. . . ."[17]

One sister in Peru strove to develop the virtues spoken of by Elder Hinckley. On one occasion, she showed she had achieved them to a remarkable degree. By being in tune with the Spirit, she was able to lift another. Although the incident took place in the house of the Lord, we can believe that when this woman goes to her home, she will, as Joseph Smith exhorted, "let kindness, charity, and love crown [her] works."

A temple president related that one day in the temple this sister, with whom he was not then acquainted, was looking about, seeming to not know just where she was to go. He asked if he could help. She replied, "No, but can you hear the choir singing?" He could not. But knowing that she could, he stood and listened intently until he, too, could say that yes, he could hear it. It was a blessing that he, although the temple president, would have missed but for a devoted sister who shared her faith and her experience.

Bishop Sylvester Q. Cannon told Relief Society women: "I do not believe you really know how powerful your influence is; and if you do begin to appreciate how important it is, I am sure you will realize the care that should be exercised in all that you do in your official capacity."[18]

President Hugh B. Brown said: "We call upon the Relief Society . . . to continue to build bridges which unite individual hearts, unite people, groups, and nations and thereby help to establish universal peace. . . . There never was a time when conviction and dedication were more needed than now."[19]

The way we do this is through love. This is what the Savior did, and what he taught all who would become his disciples. Love is in fact the identifying quality by which we can be known as followers of Christ: "By this shall all men know that ye are my disciples, if ye have love one to another" (John 13:35).

President Brown also said: "There is a drawing power in love. You can feel it just as surely as you can feel heat or cold. 'I will draw all men unto me,' said Jesus. Whenever you come into the presence of a loving heart, if you are in tune, you will feel the heavenly power and will be drawn by the magnetism of love. Service is included in, and is a product of love."[20]

10

To Love Is to Serve

So long as we love, we serve.

—*Hugh B. Brown*

*I*n a list of four important advantages Relief Society participation holds for the sisters of the Church, Elder Gordon B. Hinckley included "subduing self."[1] While knowledge, faith, and hope may be achieved through personal efforts, interaction with others is desirable for subduing self. Elder Bruce R. McConkie said, "Service is a matter of getting out of ourselves and getting into the lives of other people, of touching the hearts."[2] Evidence that this is happening can be seen in the lives of many women who give the kind of selfless service, cloaked in Christlike love, that is the manifest charity with which Relief Society is identified.

President Hugh B. Brown reinforced this idea when he said: "The inevitable expression of real Christianity is a life of sacrificial service."[3]

One of the most difficult times to help another is during a terminal illness. For so long the person has been sustained through hope and faith until, finally, despite all that can be done, the course of the disease is not stayed. One woman found that being very available to her sister-in-law during her last two years of a struggle with cancer opened opportunities for helping that might not otherwise have been possible. Although many times putting the needs of her sister-in-law before her own meant sacrificing other activities she might have pursued, she believed it was the continuing support she could give by taking her to each visit with the doctor, staying through her treatments, calling daily, sewing together, and planning family get-togethers, that enabled her to have both the relationship and the proximity that allowed for the service that was needed. They had talks about death, for example, and comforting discussions about eternal relationships. Although the sister-in-law was not a member of the Church, she was able, through their conversations and through her sister-in-law's loving service, to learn gospel truths that prepared her for further spiritual growth.

The two had good times together with their sewing and craft projects, and although each one knew that their earthly association would be unavoidably short, they made the hours and days they had happy ones. When death did come, the sister cherished memories and the knowledge that she had been able to truly help. This she could do because she had made herself available for service. She loved her sister-in-law, and her sister-in-law knew it.

President Brown said: "Let this ever be our prayer as we labor in Relief Society: 'Help us, O Lord, to find those who need us.' . . . Let everyone get under the load of responsibility, and realize that every doctrine has its associated duty, that every truth has its task. The gospel when the Master first proclaimed it, was not intended primarily for preaching—it was intended for action."[4]

When President Brown declared that we need to "realize that every doctrine has its associated duty, that every truth has its task," doctrine and truth were essential factors in those equations. Living the life of a Christian fulfills the law, but knowing the law fully is also necessary. In a Church where a principal pillar of belief is continuing revelation and where knowledge is prized as a necessary component of perfection, learning is crucial. It is the wellspring of the vitality that so characterizes the Latter-day Saints. Continuous study keeps us at the cutting edge, helps us to be honed for the work, able to know where our effort fits into God's program and close enough to his Spirit to receive working directions.

President J. Reuben Clark, Jr., emphasized the importance of knowing the Lord's will when he said:

> If you are to do this work in accordance with His will there must come into your hearts love unbounded; there must flow through your souls charity, charity for the weaknesses of others, and as you will have observed, the weaknesses of others appear at no time so clearly and with so much force as in times of trouble and distress; it is in such times that lack of courage appears. It is then that defects of character are manifest; it is then that all of the unloveliness of human kind is likely to come to the fore. . . . Every day should be approached with prayer in your hearts and a determination to see not the bad but the good, for there is no one born of woman who is so depraved that there is not in him or her something of good. . . .
>
> . . . Your duty must be, as was the duty of the Samaritan of old. You must not only bind up the wounds as they exist, but you must see to it that those who are in sorrow and dire straits shall be taken care of until they shall be fully recovered. And if you will do this you will literally, my brothers and sisters, literally become an ensign to the world.[5]

On a short commuter run, twenty-four passengers were finally tucked into the small plane for the forty-five-minute trip to Chicago. Among the group were three Relief Society women taking this connecting flight on their way back to Salt Lake City. Another of the passengers was a young mother with two small children and a large diaper bag. One child was a baby she carried in her arms, the other a toddler.

A flight on a small plane, full to capacity, is tight and less than comfortable in any case. With fretful children it becomes a challenge to even the mildest temperament. This mother was trying, unsuccessfully, to quiet her two girls. The toddler had squirmed out of her seat belt and was getting very dirty on the mud-tracked floor as she lay stretched out, crying at the feet of her mother. The mother, busy caring for the baby, was not able to comfort her or to put her back in her seat.

The crying of the children unsettled the mother and annoyed some of the passengers. Others pretended not to be disturbed. But one woman *did* something. She was one of the three Relief Society sisters. Despite her own impeccable appearance and the fact that she had hours still to travel, she reached over and picked up the untidy toddler, who by now was almost to tantrum stage with her sobbing. The sister lovingly cared for her, comforting and amusing her for the remainder of the flight. As the plane arrived in Chicago, the sister continued with the young mother, taking the little girl by the hand. She retrieved their luggage, then saw them safely on their next flight.

Wherever the mother with her two little girls was going, her trip was made easier because of a beautiful woman in an impeccable pink dress who was not afraid of its being soiled with the dirty hands of a tired and fretful little child. The mother's life may forever be a little brighter as she remembers the woman who cared more about another's problems than about herself.

"To the Master," said President Hugh B. Brown, "religion meant graciousness and magnanimity, self-forgetfulness and self-denial, high purpose and deep joy in the ministry, boundless brotherhood and love blocked by no ingratitude or sin. There was inexhaustible goodwill in all of his teachings, and he emphasized over and over again the need and blessing of service—outgoing service to all those whose lives we touch."[6]

Many lives can be touched and influenced for good when we serve others with obvious concern for their welfare. A lovely Japanese sister explained how she learned to be graceful and effective in helping others. She said that as a child she was continually in the presence of her grandmother and by example learned to do just what the grandmother did. "In Asia," she said, "serving is not a training, it is the culture." And the culture teaches people to try to anticipate the need of someone. For example, when she was a young girl, if a person came into her home to conduct business, she immediately handed that person a pad of paper and a pencil, before one was requested.

She said: "Kindness is a desire to serve; if I can be useful to other people I feel good about myself. Service is one of the great gifts."

Of course, service is also found in other parts of the world. Some families excel in it. Many times we recognize members of the same family by similarities in their appearance. But in one case, at least, two sisters were recognized by the way in which they helped another person.

In a lecture room about a hundred people, mostly Relief Society women, had gathered one afternoon. One woman's child became ill, and she quickly took the youngster into the rest room to care for her.

After a moment, a second woman sitting nearby followed, to see if she could aid the mother. She found that someone else was already helping. This woman was efficiently and kindly meeting needs. She knew without hesitation precisely what to do.

The woman watching her sensed that although she didn't know this woman, she had seen this helpful manner before. She learned that the helping woman was a sister to her neighbor. Perhaps service could not be called an inherited or a cultural trait, but it surely was a manner and attitude of helping that was so basic to the natures of these two sisters who had grown up in the same home, that the woman observing could actually recognize the resemblance. Such a commendable characteristic tells a great deal about a family, its priorities, and its regard for people.

President Brown declared: "No one can doubt the central place which service held in the life of the Savior, as it is referred to in the parable of the Good Samaritan or in that other solemn utterance where the standing of the dead before the throne of God depended upon whether they had fed the hungry, clothed the naked, given drink to the thirsty, and visited the imprisoned and the sick."[7]

Elder Bruce R. McConkie presented convincing evidence

that service to those in need is indeed recognized by the Lord as service to him:

> I shall read to you a brief statement from the journal of my father in which he speaks of his mother and of my grandmother. My grandmother, Emma Somerville McConkie, was a ward Relief Society president in Moab, Utah, many years ago. At the time of this experience, she was a widow.
>
> My father writes this:
>
>> Mother was president of the Moab Relief Society. J—— B—— [a nonmember who opposed the Church] had married a Mormon girl. They had several children; now they had a new baby. They were very poor and Mother was going day by day to care for the child and to take them baskets of food, etc. Mother herself was ill, and more than once was hardly able to get home after doing the work at the J—— B—— home.
>>
>> One day she returned home especially tired and weary. She slept in her chair. She dreamed she was bathing a baby which she discovered was the Christ Child. She thought, Oh, what a great honor to thus serve the very Christ! As she held the baby in her lap, she was all but overcome. She thought, who else has actually held the Christ Child? Unspeakable joy filled her whole being. She was aflame with the glory of the Lord. It seemed that the very marrow in her bones would melt. Her joy was so great it awakened her. As she awoke, these words were spoken to her, "Inasmuch as ye have done it unto one of the least of these my brethren, ye have done it unto me."
>
> Now, I think that the Lord first tried her faith. When he had proved her worthy by manifesting that charity which never faileth, then he gave her a glimpse within the veil.[8]

President Brown said: "Strictly speaking, our worshiping assemblies on the Sabbath day should not be called 'church service' for church service should begin on Monday morning and last all through the week."[9]

And so it did for one sister in Japan. Her service for the Church was conducted day in, day out, wherever she went. When missionaries asked if she would help them with their missionary work, she responded, "How can I help?" They explained their need to be introduced to Japanese people whom they could

teach. She recognized that introductions are a necessity with
Japanese people and so she agreed. When she said yes, however,
it was with a sincerity one seldom encounters. She believed her
help was not actually for the missionaries but for the Lord himself. She knew it was the Lord who desired the work to go forward. He who knew which persons were ready to be taught, so
she prayed for his direction.

Before leaving her home she asked for his guidance. In an el-
evator she prayed to know if any person there might be an appropriate investigator. In the market, at the grocer, at the clothing
store, wherever she went she carried this prayer in her heart.
When she found people who responded, she prayed to know
when it was right to invite them to her home, then to Church.
She prayed for her children to behave well so the visitors might
not be offended by their behavior. Her children became models
of deportment.

Her prayers were heard and answered. She "found" twenty-
seven people who eventually were baptized. When someone approached her about telling her story in the Church magazines,
she stoutly demurred: "This is a matter only between me and my
Savior. He leads me. This is his work. I am only helping his a little." (Out of respect for her wishes, reference is made to her here
only because she is not identified.)

"He that is greatest among you should not call himself a dis-
ciple of the Master until he possesses the spirit and knows the
meaning of service," said President Hugh B. Brown.[10]

Elder Harold B. Lee instructed: "The whole purpose of the
Lord in life is to so help us and direct us that at the end of our
lives we are prepared for a celestial inheritance. Is not that it? Can
you give every basket of food you give, can you give every service that you render with that great objective in mind? Is this the
way to do it in order to help my brother or my sister to better attain and lay hold upon his celestial inheritance? That is the objective that the Lord sets."[11]

The association of baskets of food with eternal life takes our
thoughts to the Savior's feeding the five thousand with a lad's five

barley loaves and two small fishes (see John 6:5–13). We see in our mind's eye the twelve baskets of fragments left over from the loaves. This becomes a testimony, not only of the power of the Lord to increase the food, but also of the abundant life he offers when we give what we have and come unto him. "Give, and it shall be given unto you; good measure, pressed down, and shaken together, and running over" (Luke 6:38).

But before there could be the abundance, the lad first had to give all he had to Jesus. He probably didn't know if he would eat at all when he gave his food. But he believed in the Savior and gave willingly. And so the five thousand were fed, and he was among them.

Over the years, Relief Society women have taken countless baskets of food to the hungry. In a sense, each time one is given in love it is reminiscent of the Savior feeding those five thousand on a hill overlooking the Galilee. He would not let the hungry go away unfed. Neither will the good women who give. And who knows but what many times there is a kind of small miracle that allows them to share with others when their own supply may be less than ample.

One woman didn't wait for misfortune. She filled a basket with pleasant things and took it to where she thought it could lift or cheer—a basket of good things from the goodness of her heart. She asked that the recipient not thank her, but rather someday fill the basket again and give it to another.

President Anthony W. Ivins described his mother as a charitable woman. He knew of her devotion and that she always gave. He sensed the goodness of her heart. He said: "The poor never passed from our door without relief, and we were not very plentifully blessed with the good things of life, either; but she fed her thousands."[12]

"Volumes could be written on what has been done by the sisters of the Church by way of supplying clothing, preservation of foodstuffs, nursing the sick, and all that relates to the care of the poor," stated Elder Marion G. Romney.[13]

Elder Harold B. Lee spoke to the women about another kind

of giving, the giving of feelings of understanding and sympathy: "This valued kind of sympathy, is the kind that I want you to exercise, . . . and that is the sympathy that is not merely trying to see another one's problems through your eyes, but it is the sympathy that tries to see their trouble through their eyes. It is the kind of sympathy that tries to put oneself in the place of the sufferer. I want you to think about that for a moment."[14]

One group of women who often do not come to our notice, but who may need our sympathy, are those incarcerated in the state penal facilities. Where sufficient interest exists, local Latter-day Saint groups organize church meetings with them, including Relief Society. Some of the inmates who attend are members of the Church, but not all of them are. They hear the lessons and special speakers, and participate in homemaking activities. Some do feel the Lord's Spirit through their attendance and are influenced by it.

Elder Lee's remarks have particular meaning for our work with these women, or even our feelings about them. "It is the sympathy that tries to see their trouble through their eyes . . . . that tries to put oneself in [their] place," he said. Most of us make some mistakes daily. Although we are rueful, we can usually avail ourselves of the way to repent and recover. *Penitentiary* is a word having the same root as *penitent* and *repent,* words which all relate to overcoming wrongdoing. But sometimes we build very high walls in our hearts to separate us from someone who repents in a penitentiary. True, we would not condone the wrong, nor even remove the actual walls that must exist at the prison. But we can try to see how hard it must be for those who are imprisoned.

One sister went to speak to a Relief Society group at a prison. She reported that the women confided to her that their greatest fear is that they may not be accepted by others.

Perhaps there is a lesson in this for all of us. Feeling a part of the group is a human need. We do not have to go far from our own neighborhoods to find people who may not feel accepted by others. A kind of service we all can give daily to those about us is to be accepting, to try to see a problem from another's perspective. Most of us already think we can do that, but we may not always take the opportunity to try. There could be sisters in our midst who for some reason feel left out. Perhaps someone is new to the neighborhood or even to the country, and doesn't yet know the customs or the people. Maybe she is not new but just different, and hasn't yet come to feel that she is a part of the group. There may be someone in our own family who does not feel that she fits in. Elder Lee was asking us to try to feel as she might feel.

The Prophet Joseph Smith said that the Lord has put sympathies in the bosoms of women and that Relief Society enables women to act according to those sympathies. Elder Lee was reminding us that charity will not fail if we do not.

President Hugh B. Brown said: "Fortunately, in the lives of many people, piety really does involve goodness, and faith involves justice, and worship, humaneness, and their life with God has a definite connection with their daily relationships. It makes them better home folk, better friends, neighbors, and citizens."[15]

Bishop LeGrand Richards related an experience a member of the Church shared with him. He felt that it illustrated the need the Lord has for people to do the work he would do. As Bishop Richards said on an earlier occasion: "Now, the Lord does a marvelous thing among his children. He provides the ways and the means and he gives us the ideas and the inspiration, but even the Lord has to have people, his children, to work out his designs."[16] The brother who told Bishop Richards about the incident said he was driving through a city when he passed a bar. He saw a young serviceman coming out of the door. He was obviously reeling from the effects of alcohol. There were women of the streets lurking about and the brother shuddered to think what was in store for this unsuspecting young boy.

Elder Richards continued:

[The man] said, "Something said to me, 'you rescue that boy.' I found a place to park my car, and went back and took the boy by the arm and said, 'You come with me,' and the woman said, 'Oh, no, you don't, he's mine.'"

And this man said, "There is a policeman right on that corner, and if you want to be turned over to him you just interfere."

She saw the policeman and walked away. He took the boy and drove him around until he sobered up, and then took him to a hotel and got him a room.

The man said to me, "I don't know why I did it. I have never done a thing like that before in my life." This good brother left his calling card with the boy, and a little later he received a letter from the boy's mother. As I recall, it came from New Jersey. She wrote: "I don't know why you stopped to help my boy that night unless it was that I prayed for him that night as I think I had never prayed for him before."

You see, God wanted to answer her prayer, but he had to have someone through whom he could answer it.[17]

This account aptly shows why love is a necessary part of service. This man had to have a great deal of love in his heart not only to have heard the prompting of the Spirit but also not to have turned away from it that night. Being in tune is being filled with love.

Although the account Bishop Richards shared involved the brother who stopped and helped the boy, as well as the boy's mother, he used it to point out to the sisters the kind of role they fill. He said: "As far as I can see, you women are the ministering angels through whom God blesses so many thousands of people, so I say, 'God bless you.'"[18]

In Bishop Richards's blessing and in the inspired words of the other brethren we can see fulfillment of the promise made by the Prophet Joseph Smith to the Relief Society women of Nauvoo. The Prophet said that the women would continue to be given inspired direction specifically for them, words that would empower, strengthen, and enable them to do the work of the Relief Society and also to fulfill their individual responsibilities. These prophetic pronouncements over the years have given Latter-day Saint women the surety of divine counsel and the evidence of godly concern.

Inspired instruction *has* come to the Relief Society, as promised, since the time of its organization. Each precept and promise, in a sense, seems whole and complete on its own. Yet taken together, they add "line upon line" to each other, leading us on into eternity.

As President George Albert Smith said in a 1948 Relief Society conference address: "We are his children. This is a part of his family that is gathered here today. How wonderful it is to know that he is not far from us, that he is all-powerful, and has promised us that if trouble comes, if necessary he will come down in heaven, not from heaven, he will bring heaven with him upon this earth and fight our battles and preserve us, and we will go on living throughout the ages of eternity. That is the promise of our Heavenly Father."[19]

REFERENCES

In the references that follow, *RSM* stands for *Relief Society Magazine.*

Prologue: In Keeping with a Promise
1. Joseph Smith, *History of the Church* 4:552.
2. Joseph Smith, *History of the Church* 4:607.

Chapter 1. The Individual Is Supreme

Chapter epigraph: Ezra Taft Benson, *RSM,* February 1950, p. 80.
1. Joseph Fielding Smith, *RSM,* January 1960, p. 7.
2. Gordon B. Hinckley, *RSM,* March 1967, p. 169.
3. Heber J. Grant, quoted by Joseph Fielding Smith, *RSM,* January 1970, p. 5.
4. Melvin J. Ballard, *RSM,* January 1939, p. 23.
5. Mark E. Petersen, *RSM,* February 1960, p. 76.
6. Ezra Taft Benson, *RSM,* February 1950, p. 80.
7. See J. Reuben Clark, Jr., *RSM,* December 1949, p. 796.
8. David O. McKay, *RSM,* December 1958, p. 789.
9. Hugh B. Brown, *RSM,* December 1965, p. 888.
10. George Albert Smith, *RSM,* March 1943, pp. 156–57.
11. Joseph Smith, *History of the Church* 5:25.
12. Marion G. Romney, *RSM,* February 1970, pp. 84–85, 87.

13. Thomas S. Monson, *RSM,* April 1967, p. 246.

14. Gordon B. Hinckley, *RSM,* March 1967, pp. 164–65, 169.

15. Ibid., p. 169.

16. Ibid., p. 167.

17. Marion G. Romney, *RSM,* February 1965, p. 89.

18. N. Eldon Tanner, *RSM,* December 1964, p. 894.

Chapter 2. Taking Hold of the Truth

Chapter epigraph: Marion G. Romney, *RSM,* February 1965, p. 86.

1. N. Eldon Tanner, *RSM,* December 1967, p. 892.

2. George Albert Smith, *RSM,* December 1948, p. 796.

3. Joseph Fielding Smith, *RSM,* January 1941, p. 4.

4. George Albert Smith, *RSM,* December 1948, p. 796.

5. Stephen L Richards, *RSM,* April 1944, pp. 195, 197.

6. J. Reuben Clark, Jr., *RSM,* December 1955, p. 797.

7. Marion G. Romney, *RSM,* February 1965, p. 90.

8. Ibid., p. 90.

9. Ibid., p. 91.

10. Ibid., p. 91.

Chapter 3. God Hath Spoken

Chapter epigraph: Matthew Cowley, *RSM,* January 1953, p. 8.

1. See Joseph Smith, *History of the Church* 5:20.

2. Spencer W. Kimball, *My Beloved Sisters* (Salt Lake City: Deseret Book Co., 1979), p. 8.

3. George Albert Smith, *RSM,* December 1948, p. 797.

4. Joseph Fielding Smith, *RSM,* January 1934, p. 28.

5. Joseph Fielding Smith, *RSM,* April 1961, p. 213.

6. Ibid., p. 215.

7. Marion G. Romney, *RSM,* February 1965, pp. 87, 88.

8. George Albert Smith, *RSM,* December 1948, pp. 836, 837.

9. Ibid., p. 836.

10. Matthew Cowley, *RSM,* January 1953, pp. 7–8.

11. Anthony W. Ivins, *RSM,* August 1927, pp. 384–85, 386, 387.

12. Marion G. Romney, *RSM,* February 1965, p. 87.

13. Joseph Fielding Smith, *RSM,* January 1962, p. 4.

Chapter 4. Living the Truth

Chapter epigraph: Joseph Fielding Smith, *RSM,* December 1966, p. 885.

1. Hugh B. Brown, *RSM,* December 1937, p. 767.

2. George Albert Smith, *RSM,* December 1948, p. 834.

3. Ibid., p. 834.

4. Heber J. Grant, *RSM,* June 1929, p. 328.

5. Ibid., p. 329.

6. Joseph Fielding Smith, *RSM,* August 1919, pp. 464, 465, 469.

7. Melvin J. Ballard, *RSM,* May 1932, p. 316.

8. Ibid., p. 316.

9. David O. McKay, *RSM,* January 1948, pp. 4–5, 6.

10. Ibid., p. 8.

11. Ibid., p. 6.

12. J. Reuben Clark, Jr., *RSM,* December 1940, p. 806.

13. George Albert Smith, *RSM,* December 1948, p. 834.

14. Joseph Fielding Smith, *RSM,* October 1943, p. 592.

Chapter 5. Home as a Holy Place

Chapter epigraph: J. Reuben Clark, Jr., *RSM,* December 1940, p. 802.

1. David O. McKay, *RSM,* December 1956, p. 806.

2. J. Reuben Clark, Jr., *RSM,* December 1940, p. 802.

3. Heber J. Grant, *RSM,* April 1932, pp. 300, 301, 302.

4. Thomas S. Monson, *RSM,* April 1967, p. 244.

5. J. Reuben Clark, Jr., *RSM,* December 1940, p. 804.

6. See *Lectures on Faith* 2:30–36, 56.

7. J. Reuben Clark, Jr., *RSM,* December 1952, pp. 791, 792.

8. Mark E. Petersen, *RSM,* January 1970, pp. 7, 11.

9. Spencer W. Kimball, *My Beloved Sisters* (Salt Lake City: Deseret Book Co., 1979), p. 17.

10. J. Reuben Clark, Jr., *RSM,* December 1940, pp. 808–9.

Chapter 6. Spirituality Comes into Its Own

Chapter epigraph: Mark E. Petersen, *RSM,* January 1970, p. 8.

1. Ezra Taft Benson, *The Teachings of Ezra Taft Benson* (Salt Lake City: Bookcraft, 1988), p. 496.
2. Feodor Dostoyevsky, quoted in *Reader's Digest,* June 1993, p. 147.
3. J. Reuben Clark, Jr., *RSM,* December 1940, pp. 806–7.
4. David O. McKay, *RSM,* December 1962, p. 880.
5. Stephen L Richards, *RSM,* December 1954, p. 791.
6. Ibid., p. 791.
7. Mark E. Petersen, *RSM,* February 1960, p. 78.
8. Stephen L Richards, *RSM,* December 1954, p. 793.
9. Mark E. Petersen, *RSM,* January 1970, pp. 8–9.
10. George Albert Smith, *RSM,* January 1950, p. 6.
11. N. Eldon Tanner, *RSM,* December 1964, pp. 892, 893.
12. Marion G. Romney, *RSM,* March 1964, p. 169.

Chapter 7. Mother—How Nearly Infinite

Chapter epigraph: J. Reuben Clark, Jr., *RSM,* December 1946, p. 801.

1. J. Reuben Clark, Jr., *RSM,* December 1946, p. 800.
2. J. Reuben Clark, Jr., *RSM,* December 1940, p. 805.
3. J. Reuben Clark, Jr., *RSM,* December 1946, p. 801.
4. Joseph Fielding Smith, *RSM,* December 1970, p. 884.
5. Ibid., p. 885.
6. Ibid., p. 885.
7. Harold B. Lee, *RSM,* December 1946, p. 814.
8. Hugh B. Brown, *RSM,* December 1965, p. 885.
9. Ibid., p. 887.
10. Spencer W. Kimball, *My Beloved Sisters* (Salt Lake City: Deseret Book Co., 1979), p. 31, italics in original.
11. Stephen L Richards, *RSM,* December 1951, p. 798.
12. Mark E. Petersen, *RSM,* January 1970, p. 11.
13. See David O. McKay, *RSM,* March 1942, p. 165.
14. Melvin J. Ballard, *RSM,* January 1939, p. 21.
15. Hugh B. Brown, *RSM,* December 1965, p. 888.
16. Stephen L Richards, *RSM,* December 1951, p. 799.

17. Mark E. Petersen, *RSM,* January 1963, p. 11.

18. N. Eldon Tanner, *RSM,* December 1964, p. 889.

19. Harold B. Lee, *RSM,* January 1968, p. 12.

20. John Donne, *The Complete Poetry and Selected Prose of John Donne and the Complete Poetry of William Blake,* the Modern Library (New York: Random House, 1941), p. 332.

21. Matthew Cowley, *RSM,* January 1953, p. 7.

22. Hugh B. Brown, *RSM,* December 1961, p. 815.

Chapter 8. Competent Mothers: The World's Greatest Need

Chapter epigraph: David O. McKay, *RSM,* January 1936, p. 4.

1. David O. McKay, *Improvement Era,* May 1936, p. 269.

2. Anthony W. Ivins, *RSM,* June 1929, pp. 321–22.

3. Ibid., p. 322.

4. J. Reuben Clark, Jr., *RSM,* December 1955, p. 792.

5. Hugh B. Brown, *RSM,* December 1965, p. 889.

6. Marion G. Romney, *RSM,* February 1965, pp. 88–89.

7. Heber J. Grant, *RSM,* October 1937, p. 624.

8. Harold B. Lee, *RSM,* February 1964, p. 85.

9. David O. McKay, *RSM,* December 1950, p. 800.

10. J. Reuben Clark, Jr., *RSM,* December 1952, p. 794.

11. Hugh B. Brown, *RSM,* September 1943, pp. 526, 527.

12. David O. McKay, *RSM,* January 1936, pp. 4, 5.

13. Hugh B. Brown, *RSM,* December 1961, p. 813.

Chapter 9. Charity—A Crown of Love

Chapter epigraph: Joseph Smith, *History of the Church* 4:607.

1. Mark E. Petersen, *RSM,* January 1961, p. 7.

2. Ibid., p. 7.

3. Gordon B. Hinckley, *RSM,* March 1967, p. 168.

4. George Albert Smith, *RSM,* March 1943, p. 155.

5. Marion G. Romney, *RSM,* February 1963, p. 86.

6. Bruce R. McConkie, *RSM,* March 1970, p. 171.

7. George Albert Smith, *RSM,* December 1948, p. 799.

8. Harold B. Lee, *RSM,* January 1969, p. 14.

9. Marion G. Romney, *RSM,* February 1969, p. 85.

10. Ibid., pp. 85, 88, 89.

11. Joseph Fielding Smith, *RSM*, January 1963, p. 5.

12. J. Reuben Clark, Jr., *RSM*, December 1940, p. 801.

13. J. Reuben Clark, Jr., quoted by Harold B. Lee, *RSM*, August 1939, p. 526.

14. Levi Edgar Young, *RSM*, March 1942, p. 157.

15. Joseph Fielding Smith, *RSM*, March 1954, p. 151.

16. Marion G. Romney, *RSM*, February 1963, p. 87.

17. Gordon B. Hinckley, *RSM*, March 1967, p. 166.

18. Sylvester Q. Cannon, *RSM*, December 1929, p. 661.

19. Hugh B. Brown, *RSM*, December 1961, p. 817.

20. Hugh B. Brown, *RSM*, December 1969, p. 888.

Chapter 10. To Love Is to Serve

Chapter epigraph: Hugh B. Brown, *RSM*, December 1969, p. 888.

1. Gordon B. Hinckley, *RSM*, March 1967, p. 165.

2. Bruce R. McConkie, *RSM*, March 1970, p. 171.

3. Hugh B. Brown, *RSM*, December 1969, p. 888.

4. Ibid., p. 888.

5. J. Reuben Clark, Jr., *RSM*, May 1936, pp. 274, 275–76.

6. Hugh B. Brown, *RSM*, December 1969, p. 886.

7. Ibid., p. 886.

8. Bruce R. McConkie, *RSM*, March 1970, p. 169.

9. Hugh B. Brown, *RSM*, December 1969, p. 886.

10. Ibid., p. 886.

11. Harold B. Lee, *RSM*, December 1946, p. 815.

12. Anthony W. Ivins, *RSM*, June 1929, p. 322.

13. Marion G. Romney, *RSM*, February 1963, p. 85.

14. Harold B. Lee, *RSM*, December 1946, p. 817.

15. Hugh B. Brown, *RSM*, December 1969, p. 885.

16. LeGrand Richards, *RSM*, February 1949, p. 77.

17. LeGrand Richards, *RSM*, February 1951, p. 80.

18. Ibid., p. 80.

19. George Albert Smith, *RSM*, December 1948, p. 839.

INDEX